A FULLY
SECURED
HEART

A FULLY SECURED HEART

My Journey To Complete
Safety And Security
In The Home Of God

Melissa Rosenberg,
PhD, LCPC

A FULLY SECURED HEART

*My Journey To Complete Safety And Security
In The Home Of God*

November Media Publishing

For permission requests, write to the author, addressed "attention: Melissa Rosenberg, PhD, LCPC," at the email address below.

melrosenberg@gmail.com

Ordering information: special discounts are available on quantity purchases by corporations, associations, and others. For details, contact the author at the email address above.

Printed in the United States of America
Published & Produced by November Media Publishing

All Scriptures quotations, unless otherwise indicated, are taken from the New American Standard Bible (NASB), King James Version, CJB, Voice, RSV, EXB.

ISBN-13: 978-1-7354542-6-9

TABLE OF CONTENTS

ENDORSEMENTS

Melissa Rosenberg is one of those unforgettable souls who blows into your life like a calm wind and an anchoring presence. I've had the pleasure of watching her grow for a few years and witnessed her follow the voice of Christ into her purpose. Her training, clinical background, and wisdom from her time in the Word of God restores balance to every environment and relationship she touches.

This book chronicling God's history with her is proof of the transformative nature of God's redemptive work on the earth. You'd never know the trauma she has been through if you met her in person today. Her very own transformation is what authenticates the power of God in her life and displays the anointing she has to support men and women who battle with mental health. In this time in history, there is a great need for voices like hers and testimonies of how a person can be healed from trauma.

As a certified trauma recovery coach and fellow trauma survivor, I find her words both inspirational and instructional when I hit times where I struggle to remember who I am in Christ. Every counselor or coach needs other counselors and coaches to support our own continued growth, and Melissa is one of those people who is gifted to support both clients and other mental health professionals alike.

I am so thankful for the hope provided through this writing, and I know it will be a part of setting the captives free.

— **Kimberly Weeks,**
CTRA-A, founder of the Kimberly Weeks Freedom Academy & Narcissistic Abuse Coach

As a pastoral leader, I have known Melissa Rosenberg since her childhood. Even from a distance, I have observed God's handiwork in her life. She has endured some difficult times, but through those fiery trials, the genuineness of her devotion has been proven (1 Peter 1:7). It has brought me great joy in recent years, seeing the woman that she has become. She is living proof of God's faithfulness, and He has certainly qualified her to impart wisdom to this generation. Her words come from a place deep inside where an authentic faith resides.

— **J. Randolph Turpin, D.Min.**
Pastor and Educator
Nashville, Tennessee

I first connected with Melissa at a scholarly counseling conference almost a decade ago. Her passion for the counseling field and her faith were evident to me from the start. After interacting at international conferences throughout the years, and becoming friends as well as colleagues, I witnessed her follow her purpose and develop expertise and knowledge that she intentionally uses to raise awareness, educate, and support others. She speaks about trauma in a way that others can understand, digest, and use to positively impact their own lives. I applaud her courage in vulnerability as she shares with the world the important truths she has learned and embraced!

— **Dr. Jill Schwarz**
Associate Professor and School Counseling Coordinator
The College of New Jersey
Author and Editor of: Counseling Women across the Life Span: Empowerment, Advocacy, and Intervention

No matter what you have done or failed to do, even if those realities are the source of your greatest regrets, God still loves you. Regardless of whom you have hurt, or how others have hurt you, God has not given up on you—and He never will. In her life story, Dr. Melissa Rosenberg declares with conviction that God wants to bring you from brokenness to blessing by way of a breakthrough only He can provide. Her story is persuasive because it is *her* story...but decades of pastoral counseling tell me it could be yours, too. If trained healers like Dr. Rosenberg can feel radically and unalterably wounded, so can you. If your heart has ever felt less than fully secured, whatever the cause, the story of her journey can lead you home. Why keep settling for life as you know it? God made you for so much more! He alone has the power to take you there: "Greater is He that is in you than He that is in the world" (1 John 4:4). Why not let Him?

— **Dondi E. Costin, Ph.D.**
  President, Charleston Southern University

How could darkness have the audacity to greet a soul that zealously snatched others out of its grasp in her everyday life? Well––it did. And it has since proven to catapult its once captive along a trajectory that has forged her to become a more empathetic, compassionate, and resilient survivor.

Laced with hope, profound candidness and vulnerability, Dr. Melissa Rosenberg shares her personal story of the calamity of being broken and the exhilaration of being found and restored in Christ. In *A Fully Secured Heart: My Journey to Complete Safety and Security in the Home of God*, you will unlock greater self-awareness and healing to aid you along your journey with God.

— **Richelle Howard**
  Lead Writer & Counselor at Chelle Shante LLC

To every person in search of a heart that is fully secure, this book is dedicated to you.

To those suffering with depression, anxiety, PTSD, and chemical and/or behavioral addictions: My prayer is that this book will help you in your journey toward freedom, to identify and restore you to the person who God created you to be.

It is for freedom that Christ has set us free. Stand firm, then, and do not let yourselves be burdened again by a yoke of slavery.

Galatians 5:1

Praise to the God of All Comfort

Praise be to the God and Father of
our Lord Jesus Christ, the Father
of compassion and the God of all
comfort, who comforts us in all our
troubles, so that we can comfort
those in any trouble with the comfort
we ourselves receive from God.
For just as we share abundantly in
the sufferings of Christ, so also our
comfort abounds through Christ.

2 Corinthians 1:3-5

FOREWORD

"So if the Son sets you free, you will be free indeed."

John 8:36 (NIV)

For several months in May 2019, before we met in person, Melissa Rosenberg and I crossed paths electronically in The One University's Facebook group at TOU Live Chicago. We actually met in the ladies' restroom and chatted for a bit. When she shared how she felt about meeting me, I was amazed and speechless. I wondered what she saw in me that I didn't yet see...

As time went on, and we engaged more online, Melissa discovered that I was offering writing workshops for new authors. She signed up and was diligent with all the requirements for the course. As she took the workshop, we chatted. As Melissa shared, I started to see changes that maybe she wasn't yet even aware of. I saw her growing and healing right before my eyes.

As Melissa progressed with the writing process, and without her knowing, I found myself praying for her. I knew that writing *A Fully Secured Heart* was taking her through mental and emotional anguish, as she had to relive some earth-shattering memories to be able to record them. As Melissa recorded them, I saw a glow come over her. As she wrote her book, her social media posts became bolder, more transparent and more joyful. God was turning Melissa's ashes into beauty - right before my eyes. I know that others noticed it, too. Her story of triumph over what should have killed her has blessed my heart every time I hear it (or read it). God has turned Melissa's mourning into joy, and the heaviness has lifted.

I am grateful that I had an opportunity to play a role in Melissa's book being written. In turn, she has had a role in assisting me in handling some personal matters of the heart, especially during this year's COVID-19 season. At dark moments, her words to me have been comforting and encouraging.

Regarding *A Fully Secured Heart*, this is a book that you won't be able to put down once you pick it up. Melissa is a naturally gifted writer, and you will visualize every moment that she is describing. Her love for people is evident, even in her writing. She has poured her heart into this book, and you will feel it. Be prepared to have a box of tissues close by as you read.

It is my prayer that every person who has the opportunity to read *A Fully Secured Heart: My Journey to Complete Safety and Security in the Home of God* will be blessed, challenged, uplifted, encouraged and set free. Melissa Rosenberg is one of a kind and this is evident in her book. Her level of transparency in this book will change your life, as it has definitely changed mine.

— **Michelle G Cameron**
   Author, Speaker, Writing Coach

PROLOGUE

"No tears in the writer, no tears in the reader. No surprise in the writer, no surprise in the reader."

Robert Frost

May 26, 2019, when I was leaving a conference in Chicago for The One University, I was crying out to God through a tear-drenched face. I was standing on the side of the road in a tunnel, outside of the bus station. I was waiting for my bus from Boston to Portland, Maine, when I pleaded with God that I needed Him to complete the healing He had begun in me, and I didn't know how He was going to do it, but He had to tell me. It was at that exact moment when I heard Him speak very clearly in my spirit, "You're going to write your way through this."

It's now August 4, 2019, and here I am beginning to write. I've put this off for as long as God would allow because I didn't know how this was going to happen. You see, I'm the type of person who, when I go for a walk in the woods I want to know the EXACT route I'm going to take, where the path begins, and where it ends. I like to try to predict the outcome from the beginning. I've done this for a good portion of my life and being a lifelong student working toward the end of achieving a PhD was a good match in this way. It's always felt safe to me, this predictability. This illusion of control. I like to try to understand things before I begin them. It's my way of attempting to take the risk out of the investment. It's been my way to try to have control and to make myself feel safe and secure. But life isn't meant to be lived this way, and writing isn't meant to unfold this way, either.

In the book *Walking on Water: Reflections on Faith and Art*, Madeleine L'Engle writes: "But one does not have to understand to be obedient. Instead of understanding—that intellectual understanding which we are so fond of—there is a feeling of rightness, of knowing, knowing things which we are not yet able to understand."

So, here I am. Taking a risk at last into that experience of knowing things that I am not yet able to understand, and writing this book because, for the first season of my life, I'm choosing to practice obedience over understanding.

INTRODUCTION

What Am I So Afraid Of?

For the Spirit God gave us does not make us timid, but gives us power, love, and self-discipline.

2 Timothy 1:7

I wonder what would happen if I told you my real story? My whole story. My raw, unfiltered, ugly, dirty, despicable story. This isn't the story that we clean up for church, or social groups, or even our friends and families. It's not the one we tell our co-workers, our peers, our teachers, and mentors, or sometimes even our therapists. It's the one we tell only ourselves, in the quiet recesses of our hearts and minds, where it's dark and hidden from all possible judgment and ridicule; except our own.

Make no mistake: I have two major enemies who have been warring against me not to write this book. The first one is my ego. My own false self-image. A major part of my work in breaking this soul tie with my false self-image and gaining freedom in the Spirit is to be honest about who I've really been, and the things I've really done. My other enemy: Satan himself. He's tried to capitalize on every one of my flaws and weaknesses to keep me from writing this book. Some of the doubts, lies, and fears he's whispered in my ear concerning the writing of this book sound like this: "If they really know who you are and what you've done, they won't respect you anymore. You'll lose all of your creditability as a counselor and as a person." Or this: "They're going to think you're crazy and unstable. Why would anyone value you or your professional expertise, after you tell them the truth about yourself?" Or this: "No one is going to care about what you have to say. It's going to be a huge waste of your time. Why even bother?" And finally, and maybe the worst, this: "They'll reject you and abandon you if you tell them the truth. It's better to keep it hidden."

Does any of this sound familiar to you? If it does, then thanks be to God that we're not alone. However, these are lies, and they need to be identified and dismantled. These are the lies I'm going to fight through because God told me that writing this book matters for my own healing journey, and God told me that writing this book matters for your healing journey. So I'm fighting not just for myself, but for you as well.

If you are holding this book in your hands right now, that is a victory that belongs to Jesus. God's Holy Spirit has given me the wisdom, grace, and courage to know that every time I show my vulnerability, my weaknesses, my flaws, and my failures to others, and highlight how God and God alone rescued me, others will be set free. No one gets free through us showing one another false self-images of gleaming perfection and seeming all-togetherness. Rather, that's a sure way to cause us to stumble—to promote comparison, jealousy, envy, discord, and further bondage. Instead, we all get freed by sharing our own ugly truths from where we once came and leading others straight to Jesus who is the Only One who is worthy of the Glory, because He's the Only One who paid the price, and died for it.

I've enlisted people to be praying for me as I write this because I know whenever we step into something that God wants us to do, the enemy stakes a battle against us. As I write this book, I'm going to put on my armor daily, and I'm going to reach out to others whom I trust to put it on for me when I feel too weak to do it myself. I'm going to remind myself of the truth of the scripture that says: "No weapon formed against me shall prosper." And I'm going to humble myself every time I step up to this manuscript and ask the Holy Spirit to write this book for me and through me because, without Him, I can do nothing. But with Christ, all things are possible.

1

The Steel Box In My Heart

At that moment their eyes were opened, and they suddenly felt shame at their nakedness. So they sewed fig leaves together to cover themselves.

~ Genesis 3:7

I was in the second grade. I don't remember how it happened, but I remember the laughter from the boys seated behind me. I was on the floor, and the wave of emotion went through my body with the power of the greatest ocean wave, and I was drowning. The humiliation and shame were so intense I thought for sure I would die right then and there. But that would have been so much less painful. Instead, I had to get up. I stood up from the broken chair, feeling the sharp pain of the fall on my backside. I quickly glanced at the row of desks behind me and zeroed in on the faces of two boys mocking me: "She's so fat she broke the chair." That's all they had to say. My worst fear, spoken aloud, for everyone to hear. My most hated part of myself called out loudly and there was nothing I could do. Even so, in desperation, I tried to defend myself: "The leg was already wobbly," I pleaded. It's all I could muster to get out. They looked back at me with huge grins on their faces, and laughing said, "Yeah right! We know it was your fault."

And there it was. That was all it took. That one little moment. A broken chair in second grade for a girl who was already riddled with self-consciousness, insecurity, and self-loathing. I didn't know this at the time, but that interaction solidified a lie so deeply in my soul that would wreak havoc in my life for years to come. The lie was this: "You are shameful. You are disgusting. You are not worthy of love."

I took that lie, put it in a steel box, and buried it deep inside my heart. I'm 41 years old, and I've spent my entire life hiding that lie from myself and others. I've run from it and tried to escape from it with every tactic known to mankind. I've attempted to restrict my way out of it (anorexia and over-exercising); perform, strive, and earn my way out of it (achievement, perfectionism, and people-pleasing); drown it through escapism and numbing (alcohol, food, promiscuous sex, and spending money); and pretend my way out of it (co-dependency, and relationship addiction). Thankfully, there is one force that can break down even steel, and that force is fire. And guess who God is? A consuming fire! Hebrews 12:29 says, "For our God *is* a consuming fire." Can I get a "Hallelujah"?!

It didn't help my self-confidence growing up that I had a sister five years older than me who was the epitome of all I thought I lacked. Because she was five years older, I literally spent my entire life looking up to her. She looked the way I had been taught by my culture that beauty should look: like one of the Barbie Dolls in my collection. When I looked at her I saw perfection. She was everything I wasn't. She was tall, blond, and blue-eyed, with tanned skin, a gorgeous smile, and an incredible figure. Did I mention she was also incredible at sports and a stellar student? Yeah, no pressure there. Against my dark hair and eyes, humongous dark eyebrows, heavier frame, and pale white skin, I remember thinking when I compared myself to her: "I'll never be good enough. I'll never measure up." I secretly wondered if she was ashamed of me. It might not have been true, but it didn't matter; it's how I felt. And isn't that the way believing lies goes for us? If it feels true, it must *be true*. At any rate, it looked as if everything she did turned to gold. And I just felt like dust.

During my middle school years, there was a major shift between 6th grade and 7th grade. I developed some super-weird form of "chronic hives." I honestly still call it that because the doctors never told me or my mother any other term. All I know is that I was covered for weeks with large red bumps all over my arms, legs, and trunk of my body and no primary care doctor could figure out why. In time, I was referred to an allergy specialist, who laid me face down on the table, opened the back of my johnny, and proceeded to pour tiny droplets of all sorts of liquids on my back that contained active properties of things that people are often allergic to. Among them were cat dander, dust, and certain foods. The next step in this procedure involved taking a tiny needle and pricking the area on my skin where the certain liquid was to see if I would have an allergic reaction. During this treatment, the doctor discovered that he thought I was allergic to "red dye." This actually made sense to my sixth-grade brain, given all of the popsicles I ate on a daily basis! The course of treatment was to limit my diet to whole foods and to wait to see if the hives would go away.

So I went home and my mother cooked plain poached chicken, steamed broccoli, and rice for me for about two weeks. It was not the most exciting diet in the world, but the hives went away! The other thing that disappeared was about 20 pounds! Limiting my diet to whole foods and cutting out junk food completely transformed my early adolescent body. It was not planned this way, at least in my mind. However, I realize looking back, that God allowed me the blessing of stepping into the rest of middle school and high school with a healthy body and a much greater degree of confidence. The problem was, I still had the steel box in my heart. I just looked different on the outside.

As I went through high school, I developed a love of being active and I played three sports a year: soccer, swimming, and tennis. This was fun for me, and it also kept the weight off. I also was involved in other extracurricular activities, such as chorus, "select chorus"—the chorus for the 'real deal chorus people"—theater club, the school musicals, the environmental club, key club, and, of course, vice president of my class...remember the over-achiever part? I had a lot of friends, enjoyed my activities, and had an all-around pretty great experience in high school. Even though I was busy in high school, and began to move away from youth group activities at church in replacement for school activities, I was still a good kid. I didn't drink or do drugs. I didn't even have sex. I was what you might classify a "goody-goody." I was one of those kids who actually enjoyed high school. I know; it's weird.

I even had a steady boyfriend. He was two years younger than me, but still in my circle of friends due to common extracurricular activities. We started out as "just friends," but ended up dating after confessing to each other at my junior prom while slow dancing that we "liked each other." While I didn't see anything wrong with our relationship at the time, I knew somewhere deep down that there was something off. He was highly charismatic and fun, but also highly volatile and emotionally immature. I am convinced, on the other hand, that I had been an adult since birth...always concerned about doing the right thing, and taking care of others.

During our relationship, my mother became clinically depressed for the first time. When our family, meaning my father, my older sister, and I, checked my mother into the psychiatric hospital, my boyfriend was with me. There is an image imprinted on my brain of seeing her sitting in a chair in the hospital in a catatonic state. I was a senior in high school. Visiting hours were over, and I had to leave my mother there. I had to leave my mother in a cold, foreign place, with mentally ill people. I felt like I was abandoning her. As the door to the unit closed firmly and was locked behind me, I leaned against the wall and slid down to the floor in tears. My boyfriend was there. That moment solidified the cycle of looking to others to help me feel safe because the pain of seeing my mother so sick was too much for me to bear alone.

Our relationship went on, and I graduated from high school. My mother was too ill to attend my high school graduation party. I had dreamt of going to a private college in Florida to study marine biology and I got in, but our family couldn't afford it. I went to a university two hours from home instead. The first year of university was horribly sad for me. I was torn between making new friends and transitioning into my new college identity, and my longing for my boyfriend back home. I got through the year, but I just knew that things could not continue this way. I felt deep down inside, that he was going to break up with me. I was a virgin still and always had planned, due to my Christian beliefs and upbringing, to save myself for marriage. But I was afraid. I thought maybe if I had sex with him, he'd stay. Little did I know at the time that was the beginning of a pattern I'd repeat over and over and over again, throughout my life.

So one afternoon, the summer between my freshman and sophomore year in college, we had sex together for the first time. He was a virgin too, but it didn't matter. It hurt physically, but it hurt more emotionally. I knew why I was doing it. I was doing it because I didn't want our relationship to end. I was scared of losing him. I thought if I went through with it (my attempt to earn his forever love), he wouldn't leave me. So I did it; and I cried the whole time. Several months later we sat in my dorm room and I pleaded with him not to break up with me. But it was too late. He was already starting to date someone else. He left the room. I sobbed uncontrollably. And then I got up, washed my face, and without even knowing it, I added another layer of steel around the box in my heart.

INTERNAL VOWS

After about two weeks of broken-heartedness, during my first ever situational depression, I asked my father from the couch during the "Ice Storm of 1998" if I would ever stop feeling this way. I really thought I never would. He told me that there would be "so many men over the course of your life who will wish for the chance to love you." But at that moment, I didn't believe him. And honestly, even if that were true, my mind asked, "What would be the point, if this is where it would end up leaving me?"

So, I made a vow to myself: I would never again let *them* see and know the "real me." They could have access to my body, my time, my mind, my money, and my soul. But they would never get to my heart. This is how I would stay safe: from judgment, from pain, from rejection, and from abandonment. And with this vow, in addition to the well-fortified steel box inside my heart, I would encase my heart in steel, as an attempt to keep out the hurt and loss associated with emotional intimacy with men, I would keep out any possible good as well. And then I spent the next 20 years of my life manifesting this vow.

NEW IDENTITY

She was my best friend in college. She had bright red hair that she wore in a bob and she drove a Ford Probe. She was smart, funny, gritty, talented, generous, and honest, and just a little bit wild. She was the perfect person for me to create my new brand of identity with. I'll never forget her advice that the best way to get over my breakup was to quickly have sex with someone else. I told her I'd only ever had sex with one person. She told me it was all the more important then. I maintained being a straight-A student and president of the Sophomore Women's Honor Society by day and added in Party Girl by night. With feelings of depression still going strong, and the continuous inner dialogue of shame and guilt, I lost 20 more pounds within a couple of months. I exercised twice a day and can remember beating myself up internally for something as small as eating a muffin. I ate mini-shredded wheat cereal with skim milk for almost every meal at the school cafeteria because it was the only consistent offering that I knew had the least amount of calories, and I could keep it consistent and control it. I monitored every calorie in and every calorie out. The only calories I didn't count were the alcohol. I figured I was eating so little during the day and exercising so much that I could drink as much as I wanted to and still not gain weight. My theory proved true. I'll never forget the moment that I stepped into a size 4 and it actually fit. I'm 5'9." To my very ill brain at the time, this was victory. I was becoming someone on the outside whom I didn't recognize. This made it easier to allow for my false-identity and incongruent behaviors to the person I used to be to take shape. I looked completely different on the outside than who I was on the inside. It was another layer of safety and protection. More steel added.

I started going out to parties at fraternity houses on the weekends. There was always free-flowing alcohol and no one knew me. I could be and do whatever I wanted and it didn't matter. Or at least so I thought. I didn't realize the damage I was doing to my soul. I just wanted not to feel. I began "hooking up" with guys who found me attractive. It wasn't necessary that I found them attractive: What I craved was their attention; their validation. I wouldn't have sex with them at first. We would just make out. I often got called a "tease" but, in my mind, that was better than being a "slut." But sooner or later, with some of them, I would cave and allow sex. Most of the time I was drunk and completely vulnerable. I didn't know if they were using protection or not. I have never caught an STD, but that was only by the grace of God. Every time the next morning, I would stand in the shower and promise myself it wouldn't happen again, and then spend most of the day in the dark, in bed, in my room with deep shame, guilt, and depression. But it would happen again because the slow fog and numbness of alcohol allows you to do things that you never thought you'd do. The amount of shame and self-loathing that I racked up over those next two short years was sometimes unbearable. But by day, I was the perfect student and none of my professors or peers in my psychology program had any idea.

By the time my senior year came around, I was studying abroad in Perth, Australia. There was no place better for me to go than to an entire continent where no one knew me and I could be anyone and do anything. And I did. Most of the time I was there I dated a guy from Ireland. We had a sexual relationship but I justified it to myself because at least I wasn't with multiple people. Australia was a great place to pretend to study while you partied. No one expected much of an exchange student from America, but I still did well in my academics, not that I remember a single course I took.

The day I got home from Australia, my mother was in the midst of her first full-blown manic episode. I knew that she had been sick while I was away because she wrote me a letter that made absolutely no sense. I was angry with my father and my sister for keeping it from me, but they were trying to protect me. I remember driving to the Old Port in Portland, Maine, with my usually neat, strait-laced mother in the passenger seat. She was now wearing a tie-dyed t-shirt, looking sweaty and disheveled, and yelling out the window. She was having fun and laughing, but I was terrified. I wanted my mom back, and she was nowhere in sight even though she was right beside me. She bought me a pair of bamboo earrings at Mexicali Blues, and later that day, we checked her into the hospital.

That weekend I went to a party at a friend's apartment and got drunk. I met a guy who walked me to the store to get more beer and by the end of the night I was in his bed. What I thought was going to be a one-night stand, ended up being a three-year relationship. It was convenient, because he was there, and he never judged me or my family situation. We honestly had very little in common when it came to life goals and education. What we had in common was chemistry. We spent three years having sex, drinking, smoking pot, and eating. We went to church together sometimes, so I figured it was okay. He introduced me to pornography for the first time. At first, I was upset and felt belittled and jealous, but then I accepted it as normal. As much as our relationship allowed the enemy to run rampant throughout my life, he was the first guy since my high school boyfriend who I actually let see me. I broke my vow with him. I let him in. But that was only because I was sure he wouldn't leave me. I knew he loved me more than I loved him and I thought that he was more broken than I was, so I assessed that he was emotionally safe. Added to this, he had his own apartment and I could go there anytime. I was working as an educational technician in a special education classroom with children who had mental health issues, learning disabilities, behavioral concerns, and major trauma backgrounds, and I was living in my parent's basement apartment, so as usual, it was convenient to have a place to escape.

FALLING

I had broken up with my boyfriend just months before, not because I didn't love him but because I knew I'd never marry him. I knew God wanted me to surrender that relationship and had plans for me to go to graduate school. And I also knew that my boyfriend was never going to pursue goals and dreams of education and career as I was. I was terrified that if I lived with him, I'd end up marrying him and having a baby, and then I'd never pursue my career goals. So one day I fell down on my knees and agreed with God. I would surrender the relationship. But in return, He had to show me His love, because I couldn't do this alone.

It was now June 2004, and I had just completed my first year of graduate school for clinical mental health counseling. I was in counseling myself at the college counseling center and taking antidepressants for the first time. My counselor told me she believed it was a "situational depression" brought on by my recent breakup. The stronghold of rejection continued for me. I have never been able to end a relationship without getting depressed.

I spent most of my time studying and saw close friends occasionally. It was the weekend of the Old Port Festival. I didn't want to go. I wasn't in the mood to be around other people and I was feeling anything but festive. At the time, my sister was still married and she was in Portland with her then-husband. I told both of them I didn't want to go, but her husband persuaded me. I can remember standing on the curb with them in front of my parent's home, waiting for the taxi that would take us into town. I still didn't want to go. But I didn't have the courage to stand up to him and tell him no. So we headed to the festival.

I never felt comfortable around him. I always felt like I had to be guarded and somehow prove myself to him. As we proceeded through the day, we went to many restaurants and performances, and along with each stop came the consumption of more alcohol. Once I opened the flood gates that day, the alcohol washed over my brain and I lost all control. I don't know how much I drank, and have little memories of the day, except for our final stop.

It was a tall brick building on one of the most prominent corners of the Old Port—the corner of Exchange Street and Fore Street. At that point in the evening, my sister and her husband were ready to leave, but I remembered that I had been invited to a "penthouse party" in this building and insisted that we go. I don't remember getting up the many flights of stairs, but I do recall being at the door to the apartment and knocking, only to realize that no one was home.

And then came the moment that could have ended my life forever. As I turned to leave, I pushed open a door that I assumed was a door to a corridor, only it was not. It was a door to a fire escape. The rest I don't remember. My next memory was lying on the ground, and hearing my sister screaming in terror somewhere above me. It was pitch black, and I could hear her yelling to her husband to call 911. I've never heard my sister sound more terrified in my entire life and this panicked me. I could hear her coming down the fire escape. The sound of her voice was piercing. I had no idea what had happened, but I knew there was a good chance at that moment that I might die. I remember my sister being over me and continuing to tell me not to move. The only thing I could say is "I'm okay." I said it over and over again. It was as if I'd believe it myself if I convinced her.

The next flash of memory I have is being in the hospital. I was lying on a table and they were cutting my favorite jeans off of my body. My mother was there and she was holding my head in her hands. Again, I was terrified. I knew my head was bleeding and I had no idea if I would survive. They put stables in the top of my head in the shape of a cross. I still can feel the impression on my skull to this day of where the fracture occurred. It used to scare me. Now it serves as a reminder of what God did for me.

The next memory I have is waking up throughout the night in the sterile room of the hospital. My room was dark and, although I could hear nurses talking nearby in the hallway and see faint light coming in, in that hospital bed I was all alone. I've had many sleepless nights in my life and this night would rate as one of the very worst. The depth of fear I had as I lay there was profound. Not only did I realize that my neck was in a cast, but I was so badly bruised all over my body that the slightest movement sent shock waves of pain. I called out for a nurse to ask for ice chips. I wondered if I would ever be able to walk again? Would my brain ever be the same? Would I be able to think as I always have? Would I still be "smart"? Would I finish graduate school? I had no answers to any of these questions. It was just me, alone, in the hospital bed. Just me and God.

Early in the morning, I was awakened by a neurologist and a team of resident doctors standing around my bed. The neurologist explained different medical procedures and possibilities to the team, of which I understood little. However, this is what I do recall: The team of doctors left the room, and before the neurologist followed them, he looked me straight into the eyes and asked me this question: "What the hell are you doing here?" The question was at once startling and relieving. I knew exactly what he meant. He was telling me that I shouldn't be alive right now. He was saying that people don't survive three-story falls off buildings onto rubble in alleyways. He was confirming the fact that my being alive at that moment was nothing short of a miracle. Then he turned on his heel and walked out of the room.

I lay in the bed, stunned. Directly following, me, the girl who had forever doubted her worth, heard these exact words in my Spirit: "This is how much I love you." It would be years after this event, and after much more trauma, that I would come to believe that these words are actually true. That truth is this: God chose to save my life that night because of His Great Love for me. Some of us take a little bit longer than others to understand this and I'm one of those people. But God is gracious and longsuffering and His love never gives up on us.

When I think back on the accident that night, many things stand out to me, but one thing I often think about is that several months after my fall I shared my testimony at my local church. A dear sister in Christ, who was the leader of our worship team, came up to me afterward and told me that the very night I had fallen, God had woken her in the middle of the night and had told her to pray. She told me that she had no idea who she was praying for, but she did pray. Now, in this moment of sharing my testimony, it had become very clear to her: God awakened her that night to pray for *me*. I recognized that instant that God not only uses others to accomplish His will in our lives, God also uses others to save our lives.

The other memory that stands out in my heart and mind is how, directly following the accident, my body was so sore and bruised all over that it was excruciatingly painful even to roll over in bed. My mother would come into my bedroom, and physically help me into and out of my bed and help me to roll over and get as comfortable as possible. One evening when she was in my room, I shared with her the mental difficulties I had been having about the fall. I told her that I was having difficulty falling asleep because the events of the accident would replay in my mind over and over. I was also having nightmares about the accident, and waking up in a panic early in the moment, asking myself all of the "what if" questions. What if I had died? What if my brain wasn't okay? What if I had been paralyzed? That night my mother sat down at my bedside, put her hand on my forehead, and prayed Psalms 4:8 over me: "In peace I will lie down and sleep, for you alone, LORD, make me dwell in safety." After that night, the PTSD symptoms associated with the accident that were impacting my sleep never came back.

Several years later, I found myself in a "situationship" with a man whom I'll call "my warm-up narcissist," who of course, I was never supposed to be with. After a year, the night before I ended it, God gave me the word, "Ardent." The definition of *Ardent* is: enthusiastic; passionate; fiery; hot; burning; shining; glowing. Holy Spirit told me that *this* is the way Jesus loves me: Ardently. The flame of His Great Love was working against the steel box once again.

2

A Wedding Never A Marriage: How Failure Was The Best Thing That's Ever Happened To Me

The thief comes only to steal and kill and destroy;
I have come that they may have life, and have it to the full.

~ John 10:10

If you have struggled at all with self-worth and self-esteem issues as I have, then you most likely already know that striving for approval and validation and attempting to earn love (especially your own) are two of the most familiar behavioral patterns in your arsenal. I have been an expert at these patterns for most of my life. I've habitually felt extremely uncomfortable when I interpret that someone might be the slightest bit unhappy or displeased with me and the anxiety has become even worse when I have to express that I can't or don't want to do something that they desire. Welcome to People Pleasing 101. Please kindly take your seat in the front row with a perfectly sharpened pencil and a fresh notebook.

It's important to highlight in this course that people-pleasing is not just limited to other people but is also characterized by a strong inner drive to live up to one's own self-imposed preconceptions of who one believes they are *"supposed to be."* The lessons in this course are also vehemently opposed to any inkling of the risk of weakness, failure, or disappointment. Surely, avoiding feeling the weight of these '*inner demons of deficiency"* is the deepest root of perfectionism. If one can *just* control and manipulate *all outcomes* to be pleasing to *everyone, including oneself,* there will be no need to notice the grave shortcomings within and without. Here we can see that people-pleasing and perfectionism are closely familiar spirits.

My first "failure" came in college when I realized that I didn't actually want to study geology. I had it in my mind somehow (although no one in my family ever told me this) that, to be successful, I needed to pursue a career in the "hard sciences." Since the major of environmental science was not offered at my university, I chose geology because I figured that had to be somewhat similar! I soon learned that I wasn't nearly as interested in rocks as the other students in my classes. Also, I failed my first calculus class, even though I was that girl who stayed after class *every* day in an attempt to get extra help from the professor. I would look at the professor after class as I stared at my calculus book with a glazed-over look on my face and nod my head, all the while having absolutely no idea what he was talking about. I was also struggling in chemistry class. Knowing that these were the first math and science classes in a long list of upper-level courses, I became fairly certain that this was not the path for me.

I soon realized I would have to make the call home to explain this situation to my father. My parents had not attended a four-year university and I desperately wanted to make them proud and not squander my opportunity that they had both sacrificed so much for. I was truly afraid that I would be letting my parents down by telling them I thought I'd chosen the wrong major. I was afraid of being a failure. And being a failure was the worst thing I could imagine.

I called my father and told him of my struggle. I will never forget his words to me over the phone: "This is not a failure. College is about figuring out what you *are* interested in. What is it that you like to do, Melissa?" I waited a moment, and my answer came to mind readily: "I like to talk to people." His reply to me was just as fast: "Okay then, you need to start enrolling in classes that are focused on working with people." I felt my heart breathe. My father had just freed me to do what I knew I was created to do: To help people directly. I will forever be grateful for my father's confirmation of my calling that day in 1997 on the phone in my dorm room. And because I am my father's daughter and proudly take after his corny sense of humor, I always tell people that I found my path in life by one day realizing that people *really are* more interesting than rocks!

I started taking classes about people. I took sociology and anthropology. Then I landed in my first psychology course and I was hooked; I knew this was it! I decided in a lecture hall during the first abnormal psychology class of my undergraduate career that I could do what the professor in the front of the classroom was doing. I could stand up in front of hundreds of students and teach. I really enjoyed learning about why people are the way they are and behave the way they do. I realized that my empathic ability that I've had since childhood but didn't have the words to describe—the ability I have to read people's inner emotions and challenges and respond helpfully—was actually a match for this professional field. From there, I decided that I'd become some type of doctor in the field of psychology and I didn't stop until I arrived there.

This was an excellent match as well because one of the best places for people-pleasers to thrive is in doctoral programs. Consider it: The entire experience is set up to prove yourself worthy of the PhD. It was a natural fit for me and I excelled as a doctoral student and teaching assistant. I started my doctoral program when I was 30 years old. My goal was to complete the coursework, do my research, and defend my dissertation by the time I was 35. I did it all on time with a 4.0 GPA. Check, check, and check. Perfect plan executed!

Of course, I did learn a great deal during these five years as a doctoral student. I'm grateful to have had the opportunity and I use my education daily. However, the idea that once I had the Ph.D.—for others, it might sound something like once I have the job, the marriage, the house on the hill, or the baby—*then* I'll be satisfied with myself and my life, and feel complete. And of course, this is *never* the case. I've come to recognize the pattern that, as soon as we get one goal accomplished, the next one is waiting for us! So long as we ground our self-worth and contentment in external factors, circumstances, and achievements, experiencing contentment and satisfaction will always be a moving target.

Truth be told, I didn't actually *feel* any different once I had earned a PhD. Shockingly, I was still the same person, just with three extra letters after my name! This is what Harvard psychologist Tal Ben-Shahar refers to as the *arrival fallacy*. In his book, *Happier: Learn the Secrets to Daily Joy and Lasting Fulfillment*, Ben-Shahar explains this temptation to focus on the achievement of goals in order to win happiness in the following way: "We learn to focus on the next goal rather than on our present experience and chase the ever-elusive future our entire lives. We are not rewarded for enjoying the journey itself but for the successful *completion* of a journey.

Society rewards results, not processes; arrivals, not journeys" (Ben-Shahar, 2007, p. 19).

Essentially, the arrival fallacy is the *illusion* that we will attain lasting fulfillment only once we attain particular goals, and Ben-Shahar's research suggests this to be untrue. Rather, he points to our actual satisfaction as being in the *process and progress* toward our goals, as well as a practice of having gratitude along the way, not in the outcomes themselves.

This is a fun idea, isn't it? It's one of those concepts that could and would completely change our mindsets and entire lives if we decided to buy into it fully. However, striving while believing "I'll finally be happy once I make it" is so tantalizingly deceptive that it's a tough habit to quit. Most of us prefer to stay on the familiar hamster wheel of achievement addiction and perfectionism, even though in our heart of hearts we suspect, and even secretly hope, there may be a better way. In time, through the grace of God, I have come to realize that the most powerful way to impact the lives of others is not through our pursuit of perfection. Rather, lives are radically changed through sharing a glimpse of our story in the midst of brave imperfection.

I "MADE" IT

So, there I was: thirty-five years old, with a bright, shiny doctoral degree. Make no mistake, God brought me through that process. Researching, conducting, and defending a dissertation was one of the most challenging experiences I've ever gone through. But now what? I was trained to work as a counselor-educator, teaching master's level counseling students. Just as I was preparing to graduate, God opened up a door for me to work back in Portland at the very university where I had earned my master's degree. I applied for the job, interviewed, and was offered the position. I defended my dissertation in August 2013 and started my first full-time teaching position at the University of Southern Maine in September of 2013. Needless to say, it was a very short period in which to transition and I was completely exhausted when I began.

However, my next goal was already on the horizon: the ever-elusive marriage and children. I already knew for certain that I was "behind." While I was working on my PhD, my two best friends from undergraduate school had already got married and started their families. I remember having seen the two paths diverge as if in a clear picture in my mind. I was headed down the road of my lifelong dream to further my education and earn my PhD, and everyone else I knew and loved was heading down the wedding aisle. Many more of my friends since then had joined them. Thirty-five was feeling older by the minute. Aren't all of those research studies about difficulty with pregnancy geared toward women thirty-five years and older? I felt confident (enough) that I'd secured all of my future professional goals with three degrees and a university job. Now I thought the rest of my life could finally open up to me and I could actually have an authentic personal life as well! I was excited to leave the dusty stacks of the library behind, and enter back in the world of dating.

What better way to get a beat of the landscape back in the city of Portland than to join an online dating platform? Little did I know that narcissists flock to online dating sites. It makes sense, doesn't it? It's easy to be anyone when no one knows you. However, I had not one clue about this phenomenon at that point in time. This is not to say that there are not exceptional men dating online. However, as my story played out, those were neither the men I was attracted to nor the men I attracted. My first "match" was the man I married. I didn't waste any time finding the absolutely wrong one.

MY LIFE-CHANGING MISTAKE

He was a smooth talker and showed an overwhelming amount of forthcoming interest in our first couple of online conversations. He quickly invited me to meet him in person. When I arrived at the lounge of the restaurant where we were meeting, he was already seated with a bowl of chowder and a drink. Granted I was running a few minutes behind as I typically do, but I remember it striking me as odd and a little bit rude that he wouldn't have waited for me to place an order. Looking back upon things now, I see how, from the very first moment of our first interaction, God was giving me an opportunity to get out of this, but I didn't have the discernment to see this at the time. So instead, I introduced myself, sat down, and ordered a dirty martini. Mistake number two. If you are trying to get to know someone, don't use substances that alter your perception of reality. But again, at that point, I was more interested in easing my experience of social anxiety on a first date than I was in discerning God's voice.

The moment he opened his mouth to begin communicating with me, I was shocked. He had an accent and he had not disclosed online that he was from anywhere other than New York. After some time, he shared with me his real name, saying that he went by a different name online. He said that this was his "American name" that he has gone by since living in New York but that he was actually Jewish and Israeli. Although I was taken aback, I did not want to appear rude or somehow close-minded. I also was slightly intrigued, as I enjoy people from various backgrounds and I was currently teaching a course about multicultural counseling. And truth be told, I've always been attracted to foreign men.

As the date progressed, he shared that he had been married and was currently separated. Again, not wanting to judge, and thinking it was rude not to keep an open mind, I listened as he told me the story of his soon-to-be ex-wife, how difficult it had been to live with her and to parent her son from a previous relationship. All of the blame was put onto his ex-wife, and he played the victim well. Although this should have been another red flag, I actually began to feel empathy for him, that he had got into a bad situation. Before the night was over, we were snuggled up together near the fireplace and he kissed me. The chemistry was real, and

I was hooked. When we left the establishment that evening, there was a snowstorm outside and we laughed together as we cleared the freshly fallen snow from our cars. I remember wanting to continue to another establishment, but he said we should go home because the snow was getting deep at that point. I drove away thinking this romantic snowy evening fireside first date only happens in the movies and I thought that he *must be the one.*

Over the course of the next week, we texted and talked continuously and he quickly told me he was interested in marriage and children. It was as though he read my mind. More likely, he repeated back to me exactly what he thought I wanted to hear. He brought red roses to my parent's home where I was currently living. He took me out for nice dinners with drinks. He bought me jewelry. It all felt like a fairytale romance. And that's exactly what it was: all show, no substance. One evening when we were out, he appeared to be in a strange, aloof mood most of the time. At the end of the evening, he told me that he had to tell me the truth about something. He told me that he had been married not just once, but twice before. He continued by telling me that his first wife had been severely mentally ill and had ended up being hospitalized in a psychiatric ward due to her own issues of wanting to harm herself. He continued by saying how difficult it had been for him to lose her, but she wanted him out of her life and he couldn't save her from herself. He apologized for not being completely truthful with me but said he was afraid that I would run away if I had known the truth in the beginning.

I can remember the exact moment when the two paths were laid out for me. God was giving me another opportunity to escape the profound suffering that He knew was coming for me. We were standing in a hallway outside the restaurant bathrooms, with mirrors on the walls and expensive bouquets on the tables. I took a split-second in my mind, and the thought came into my head that Jesus would forgive him. My mind didn't perceive that Jesus would have boundaries and be able to discern right from wrong and judge accordingly. It was that Jesus would forgive. This is proof that my understanding of the fullness of who Jesus actually is was much more limited at the time. I put myself and my better judgment aside. I didn't protect the treasure I am because I still didn't know what a treasure I was at that time. I dropped my sense of right from wrong and my boundaries. I stuffed my intuitive voice deep down within, and I stepped into the role of the martyr. I told him I forgave him and still wanted to be with him. I made my oath then that I would be with him. At that moment, I had made my choice and there was no looking back. And he knew it.

From that time in January, things quickly ensued between us. I began spending more of my time after work at his rented cottage by the beach. We'd prepare lavish dinners after work, with cocktails. It was an absolute escape from my day-to-day life of teaching at the university and living at home. I didn't realize it at the time, but it was all an escape for me. I thought I could escape my current life by escaping into something shiny, flashy, fun, and new. I've since realized that escapism never leads to a sustainable future. But I didn't know myself then as I know myself now. I didn't even really know what I was trying to escape from. I just knew that his attention and company were addictive to me. I had finally found someone charismatic and fun who actually wanted to settle down and build a life together. Or so I thought.

One of the first odd things I can recall him doing was giving me the key to his cottage in a timeline that I intuitively felt was far too early. I remember he said that he wanted me to feel welcome to come over after work even before he was home. For the first several days after he made this offer, I still waited for him to be home before I went over. However, I can distinctly recall one evening when we were talking on the phone and he said to me in a tone I have never forgotten, "I would really like to come home and you'd already be here." I recall it so clearly because it was clear that he had taken me not coming over and using the key as an offense. This is a regular pattern with narcissists. Any type of appropriate boundary that you put up for yourself is seen by them as a personal attack on them. The situation with his house key was no different; I just did not understand it then. In looking back, I also recognize that he wanted the fast track to get me past the "dating" stage and into the "girlfriend" stage to make sure he'd secured me. Giving me his house key had everything to do with his manipulation and control and nothing to do with my comfort.

As time went on, I fell deeper in love with him. Although he was extremely immature at times, I also saw him as smart and capable, having lived abroad, worked in professional realms, and been "on his own" for some time. As a lifelong student, and him being four years older than me, he seemed very "adult." Being with him at the cottage felt a little bit like "playing house" and, although I knew things were moving incredibly fast, we were already talking about marriage.

This is where things get incredibly complicated. As I previously discussed, I was interested in being on the fast track to marriage and a family. The problem was: he was *still* married. He assured me, however, that things were completely done with his wife and they had been separated for months. He told me that they were now just waiting to go back to court to finalize their divorce. Anyone with any sense would have ended the relationship. But I wanted what I wanted. This is the part where I forced something into being that God never planned for me. I didn't ask God… wait, actually I did…well sort of. I prayed, "God is he the one for me?" I felt like God said back to me, "Is he the one you want?" I said "yes." God said, "So it will be." I often wondered why God wouldn't have told me to stop or say no. And then I think that it's probably because I was so stubborn and prideful that God knew I would have done what I wanted anyway. So I started to plan a wedding. With a married man. Before he'd even proposed.

Remember when I spoke about manipulating outcomes and having control? Not only was I drawn to him as a co-dependent moth to a narcissistic flame, but I also felt oddly safe emotionally in that I knew that he desperately wanted to get out of his previous marriage and jump into one with me. There was no risk in my mind for investment without payoff. Meaning that there was no risk that I'd put in time, energy, and care dating him, and then have him decide to leave me. Remember the steel box? There was no risk here of abandonment or rejection because I was going to plan this wedding for August, before he even got divorced in April. One of the biggest lessons I've learned about emotional risk is that it's actually more of a risk to choose co-dependency over the risk of being rejected by someone in a healthy relationship. But again, I had not learned that lesson yet. So plan a wedding I did.

DREAM WEDDING

I wanted this wedding to be the wedding of my dreams. And in true perfectionistic fashion, it was. I already knew where I wanted to have it: Sebasco Harbor Resort. Think historic Maine fishing village with traditional summer cottages and halls, ala "Dirty Dancing." It would be in mid-August, the height of Maine summer, and my favorite time of year. I had often gone kayaking off the coast of Sebasco and had dreamt about having my wedding there. Now my dreams were quickly becoming a reality.

I did not tell my mother that we were planning the wedding. I absolutely knew what she would say: No. My mother is the most practical person I know, and although she did not receive a formal higher education, she has a great deal of common sense. My mother would not have approved of moving so quickly. So the remedy was easy. I would just wait to tell her until he proposed. So the deception began. Not only was I betraying God and myself, but I began to betray others. I was not honest. I wanted what I wanted and I didn't want anything to stop me. Can you see how extremely dangerous a situation I put myself in?

The one time I began to doubt and question myself, or at least the one time I allowed myself to speak about it with anyone out loud, I told my sister that he'd been married twice before. I asked her what she thought. Her reply to me was, "People have lived lives at our age and we cannot expect people to be perfect." This response was enough to set my mind at ease and, because she's my big sister, she made it easier for me to squelch my own inner doubts and fears and resign myself to her viewpoint. She was essentially validating what I wanted to hear. Sometime later, my sister apologized to me for not given me a different response that day. But as I expressed earlier about God, it wouldn't have mattered. I wouldn't have listened anyway.

I wanted him and my father to get to know one another better, so I arranged a brunch at one of our favorite restaurants. After a nice meal and conversation, he left in his car and my father and I drove home in my father's car. Sitting in the passenger seat, I told my father about our desire to be married in the near future. My father is an extremely sensitive and understanding man; however, even he told me that it seemed very quick and that I should take my time. He told me it takes a year or more to really get to know someone and that there was no need to rush. I remember pleading with him, "Dad, I've already waited so long to be married. I don't want to wait anymore. Will you please just be supportive?" My father replied that he would support me, which is the answer I wanted. I have thought about that drive in the car often. If only I had listened to the wisdom of my father.

More time went by and I was in full-blown wedding planning mode. I secured the date at the wedding venue, bought my dress, ordered the most beautiful invitations, planned the decorations, secured the florist and the wedding cake, and even bought local mini-jars of jam as wedding favors with our names and the date inscribed. By the time he got divorced in early spring, the wedding was practically completely planned. The night he proposed to me, I had made a steak dinner for the two of us at the cottage. After dinner, I was sitting on the couch and I looked down at the coffee table. On the table, he had placed a bouquet of roses and, in the roses there was an engagement ring. As soon as I saw it, he was down on one knee beside me telling me that my mother had given him my grandmother's engagement ring for him, knowing that he wanted to ask for my hand in marriage. Then he asked me the words I thought I'd always been waiting to hear, "Will you make me the happiest man alive and marry me?" I began to cry and immediately said, "Yes."

The next few months leading up to the wedding were incredibly busy. I was teaching five courses at the university that spring semester and would be teaching three courses in the summer. Every bit of extra money I was making went toward the wedding. I was stressed and tired but I felt it would "all be worth it" in the end. The other issue that started to come up was where we would live. Seeing that I had just completed school less than one year ago, my plan was to be at my parent's home to try to save money; however, since all of my extra money was going toward the wedding, I had no savings at that point.

He had to be out of his winter cottage rental by June, so we together decided that renting a place to move in together in June knowing that we would be married in August was the most practical thing. My mother wanted me to stay living with them until I got married, but I was ready to move on and I wanted to secure a nice place to live. I had my heart set on renting a house in a nearby upscale town where I had always wanted to live. The rent was high but the home was the perfect size for two people and it was in an amazing neighborhood with beautiful scenic walking paths to the ocean, and private beach access. Little did I know that I would never be more miserable and terrified than I was once I was living in that house.

This was around the time that some of our first major fights ensued. I would want to move forward with decisions such as renting a home, signing up for a gym membership, choosing a wedding menu, or buying a couch, for example. He would drag his feet on making any move toward any decision. He would first withdraw and then escalate in rage, accusing me of being pushy and impulsive. It was an incredibly confusing pattern of behavior and left me continually wondering what I had done wrong. It was the subtle beginning of a pattern in which he would project all blame and responsibility onto me, so he could avoid it, as well as attempting to make me feel that there was something wrong with me for desiring consistency and clear communication. This went on for a few weeks over what house to rent. One morning I was getting so anxious as to where we were going to live, that I asked him to call his connection he'd been waiting to hear back from right then and there. He did as I asked, but I knew he was angry. When he got angry, you never knew when it would come out in bitterness, resentment, and rage later.

Later that day we were horsing around in the driveway getting ready to go someplace, and I playfully jumped on his back. He dropped me to the pavement and it was extremely painful. He told me that his back hurt and he had got off balance. It was the first time that I got *that feeling* inside. At that moment, I felt deep down that he had hurt me intentionally. It was a terrifying feeling to me, as I had never felt this before from anyone whom I had loved in my life. It was too horrible to believe that the person I was about to marry would intentionally want to cause me pain, no matter how angry or resentful he was from an earlier argument. So I stopped myself from thinking about it. It was the first of hundreds of times that this sort of thing would happen.

I learned to make excuses for him. I would say things to myself to rationalize his behavior like, "It's because he's stressed at work," or "There's just a lot going on right now. It won't always be this way," or "Maybe it really was my fault, and I'm just being unreasonable." I started noticing a pattern; Before almost any major event that I was looking forward to, such as trying on my wedding dress, going to try the food for the wedding reception, going for dancing lessons, going out for dinner, or going to an event with friends, he would pick a fight with me directly before or directly afterward. It always ended in me feeling awful during the experience or leaving a bad memory for me after the experience.

He would often harbor bitterness about something that occurred during an event, and then bring it up at a much later time. It was as if he had been saving up ammunition for when he wanted something to use against me. It started to get to the point where I was becoming hypervigilant about how he might behave in front of friends or family and wondering if they could tell. However, he very rarely, if ever, got angry in front of other people. It was always toward me when we were alone. He maintained a good image in front of other people.

We had moved in together and although we shared a bedroom, I had committed to God that I wanted to wait until we were married to have sexual intercourse. Over the summer before our wedding, he began the tactic of withholding sexual intimacy from me. Although I was starting to feel very concerned about this and felt that he was doing this purposefully as some type of punishment out of his resentment toward me, he continuously made excuses about it.

One of the times he yelled at me, I confronted him about it. I told him that if he did that again, I'd be gone. That afternoon, I received a basket of chocolate-covered strawberries at the house. It was his way of apologizing. A day or two later we had another argument and I will never forget this: he took the strawberries out of the refrigerator, stormed out of the house with them, and put them in his car, saying that he was going to take them with him to work because I didn't appreciate them. The level of rage that he was exuding over the strawberries was so intense that, at the moment, I could not even believe it was occurring. I was dumbfounded. I knew there was something very wrong. But I also thought that I was in too deep. This was my greatest mistake. It's never too late to turn around and go in a different direction. But I thought it was. And so I moved forward.

Only a couple of months before the wedding, I would go to the gym to meet with my personal trainer and listen to him tell me about happy weekends and evenings he had spent with his girlfriend. Most of my solo sessions were spent weeping over our latest fight while running on the treadmill, with my music turned up full blast. My focus was to look amazing in my wedding dress and I thought if I could run faster and hold out a little bit longer, I could outrun the horrible feeling in the pit of my stomach that I was doing something very, very wrong. I've learned since then that nothing I think I want is worth sacrificing my peace for. You can't outrun God. He's already at the finish line. Remember that whole part about Him being the Alpha *and* the Omega?

Every time we went to pre-marital counseling with the couple from church or tried to watch videos and do the homework together, it would end up in a major fight. If I could change anything, I would go back and call off the wedding. But that is not what happened. I had taught fall, spring, and summer courses during my first full-time year at the university without a break after a five-year doctoral program. I had moved myself twice in the past year and I had also moved all of his things from the cottage to the house, while he was at work. I had unpacked, organized, and decorated an entire home and I had planned an entire wedding. I was beyond exhausted. It was the perfect setup for a breakdown.

The day before the wedding arrived. I honestly am surprised I even made it that far. But I think I was so stubborn and hell-bent on having this perfect day. Perhaps I thought somehow, if I could just pull off the perfect wedding day, that everything would end up being okay. I recognize now how completely irrational that is, but at the time, I was just trying so very hard to hold it all together. I had come this far and I was going to go through with it. I had already started a routine of crying out to God in desperation from the bathroom floor on the bathmat. I asked Him for answers and signs, but none of the signs I thought I was looking for came. I wasn't getting the answers about how to heal this relationship or what I could do differently to make this work. I was getting what felt like silence from God, and yelling from him.

His mother was staying with us before the wedding. She had come over from Israel. He treated her badly as well and she put up with it. She coddled him and, in her mind, it was as if he could do no wrong. I remember calling her and asking her for advice about how to handle him. She told me not to talk with him very much when he got home from work and to make him a drink. That was my marital advice from my mother-in-law.

When I was getting ready to drive my car up to the resort for the wedding, I suggested that he not take his computer with him and he absolutely lost it on me. I got severely screamed at by him as I was about to leave for our wedding venue. I drove up by myself to the venue that day. I think I was already just frozen in fear at that time. I did not see a way out. I could have called it off then. I should have. But that's not how it played out.

I got to the wedding venue and began to unpack and prepare for the rehearsal dinner that evening. Guests arrived from all over the country and some from out of the country. It was absolutely amazing to see all of my beloved family and friends in one place. One beautiful location. It was my dream party. Unfortunately, I still had that feeling in the pit of my stomach. It was a feeling that would not go away but would worsen over time. The feeling of knowing you are about to go through with something that is incredibly wrong but hoping somehow it will turn out right. "I'll worry about that after the wedding," I told myself. I did not sleep well the night before the wedding. I did not have peace.

The day of the wedding arrived, and it was a whirlwind. I was up early to meet with my bridesmaids for preparations to get our hair and makeup done. Everything was beautiful. The bouquets were the most gorgeous flowers I'd ever seen. Huge pink peonies, pink roses, baby's breath, and soft light green lamb's ear. My dress was the most beautiful dress I'd ever seen. I really did feel like a queen. My hair and makeup were perfect. I held everything together until I saw my father. He took one look at me before he walked me down the aisle, and his eyes filled up with tears. I told him to stop. I couldn't look at him fully, or I knew I would break down.

The wedding reception was incredibly fun. It was a huge party with all of my friends and family. The only thing missing was a connection with my new husband. Throughout most of the wedding, I felt like he was already missing. The song that played as we entered the reception was "Crazy in Love" by Beyonce. It could not have been more on point. I was crazy in love. This love wasn't love at all. It was deception. I danced with my father to "Stand by Me," and tried not to cry. I felt like I was saying goodbye to my father. I sang a song to my husband with my father called "How Sweet It Is (To Be Loved by You)," and it was so much fun. I had much more fun and felt much safer with my father than with my husband. It was clear to me.

The night of the wedding we made love for the first time. It was over quickly and felt utilitarian. It was nothing I had hoped it would be. I had everything ready to make it a beautiful night. I wore the most gorgeous white negligée. I did not feel appreciated. I wanted to feel loved, but I felt more alone than ever.

We went home from the resort the next day and, as I unpacked the gifts, flowers, and cards from the car, the truth set in. This was really my life. I already felt such a huge chasm between him and me and I knew I'd made a mistake. I laid in my bed reading through wedding cards, and I came across a card from my mother. In it was the following passage from the Bible:

Love is patient, love is kind. It does not envy, it does not boast, it is not proud. It does not dishonor others, it is not self-seeking, it is not easily angered, it keeps no record of wrongs. Love does not delight in evil but rejoices with the truth. It always protects, always trusts, always hopes, always perseveres. Love never fails.

1 Corinthians 13:4-8

As I read the card while lying in bed, I began to weep. I knew that what I had just entered into had no resemblance whatsoever to this truth. I had made a horrendous mistake, and now I was trapped. What I was about to go through over the next year of my life I would never wish for anyone.

3

The Psychiatric Ward On New Years Day: What I Gained From Losing My Mind

I waited patiently for the LORD;
He turned to me and heard my cry.
He lifted me out of the slimy pit,
Out of the mud and mire;
He set my feet on a rock
And gave me a firm place to stand.
He put a new song in my mouth,
A hymn of praise to our God.
Many will see and fear the LORD
And put their trust in him.

~ Psalms 40:1-3

I grew up living on the Atlantic Ocean, on the rocky shoreline of Portland, Maine. It's the land where summer is filled with the scents of sea roses, pine trees, salty air, and hope. You have survived another long Maine winter, read—4 months minimum, 5 months average; and then all of a sudden, out of the blue it would seem, it's S-U-M-M-E-R! You race to the back of your closet to pull out your coveted L.L. Bean beach bag, grab your bathing suit and towel, your flip flops, your book, a cooler, beach chair, and your favorite water float, and you're off! You're gone to the beach or the lake and you won't have your toes out of the water or sand for the next three months during any spare moment you have, as long as you have any choice in the matter.

Now make no mistake, the North Atlantic Ocean is *cold,* even in Maine summertime. But that has not stopped me from swimming in it throughout the summer since childhood. I'm a real Mainah, after all. Not one of those who just come to enjoy the summer without all of the suffering of living in Maine year-round. We call those people the ones who are "*from away.*" Maine kids in the summer spend the entire day digging in the sand, making castles, moats, and other sand creatures and concoctions, and swimming in the cold ocean.

The waves can get big in Maine. We have a pretty awesome surfing community. One of my favorite activities as a kid (and, if I'm totally honest, still now as an adult) is jumping and riding waves, either on a boogie board or using my own body.) There is something so exhilarating about catching a big wave and riding it all the way into the shore. I could spend hours doing this.

But once in a while, you get caught under a wave and, even if it's momentary, it can be absolutely terrifying. It's that moment when you see the wave coming overhead and you know that instead of you catching that wave and being on top to ride it into shore safely, the wave is too big for you—and it's going to overpower you. With just enough time to gasp one more deep breath, you are completely submerged underwater, brought into the wave's undertow, and you become completely disorientated. You don't know which way is up toward the water's surface and which way is down, and you know you need to breathe soon, or else…you don't want to think about it. So you open your eyes, and look for the light --- and you start swimming as hard as you can toward this light, hoping and praying that you break through the barrier, and make it in time. When you break through, you are gasping for air and you look around just to make sure you really are okay. You hear children in the distance playing and laughing, you hear the seagulls. You let out a sigh as you swim to shore. You survived.

The story I'm about to tell you is the closest I've ever come to drowning. Caught in the undertow, I was sure I wasn't going to make it. I was *completely* helpless and *completely* hopeless. But somehow, by God's amazing grace and mercy over my life, I'm here to tell you about it now. I want you to know before you read this, that I prayed for *you* while I was drowning. I prayed that all of the suffering that I was going through would not be in vain and that, if I made it through, this story—my story—would help someone else. And this is God's faithfulness.

It's hard to know exactly how it occurred. My plunge into severe clinical depression was a fast decline. I now thank God that I became so sick so quickly. God forced everything to fall apart in order to rescue me. Had I not become so ill, I would not have wanted to let go. I would not have escaped a sociopath so quickly because I would have continued to be ridden with guilt, shame, and self-blame. But as it went, the most terrifying and isolating experience I have ever walked through, was really a demonstration of God's great protection and rescue in my life.

As I said before, the depression began as soon as I was home from the wedding. I knew I'd made a terrible mistake. With each passing day, his behaviors toward me got worse and worse. I was working at the university, teaching five courses that fall semester, but I would rush home to make dinner and clean the house to his incredibly high standards before he'd get home from work. There was nothing I could ever do that would be enough to avoid his constant criticism or complaints. Looking back now, I see that he acted that way in order to gain more control and power over me, knowing that I wanted to please him and make him happy. In the midst of it, it felt like I was constantly doing something wrong.

He withheld sex and any other type of physical or emotional intimacy with me. He began picking apart my physical appearance, such as commenting on my bottom teeth being crooked. He would tell me that I spent too much money, as he drove off to work in his convertible Mercedes. He continuously made me feel like a failure who was letting him down. One night, in a desperate attempt for physical intimacy, I gave him oral sex after he came home from work in our enclosed patio, overlooking the backyard. When he was finished, he told me he was going to go have a drink. I've felt used by men plenty of times, but at that moment, I felt like I had just prostituted myself to my husband. I felt degraded and humiliated, and I hated who I had become.

I was always waiting for the next thing that he would become enraged about. I spent hours researching a mattress topper for our bed and asked him if we could buy it. He agreed and then spent days yelling at me about it. The fear of future resentment from him became a constant in my mind because I knew that if he didn't get angry about something I did or said at the moment, there was a strong chance he would still save it to use against me later. I walked on eggshells. I pandered to his every need. I took emotional and psychological abuse I should have never accepted. With every day that went by, I got more and more ill. One of my best friends from college actually said to me on the phone that, with every passing day that I stayed in that toxic house with him, she witnessed me becoming sicker and sicker. It was true.

I pleaded with God to change my situation; to change him. I put oil on every doorway of my house. I went through every room and cast and commanded out demons. I wept and wailed on my knees. I made the sign of the cross over every room. I pleaded and begged God to change this situation; to rescue me from this misery. I went to a two-night prayer retreat on deliverance within marriages. A woman looked into my eyes, told me not to give up, and shared that she'd been waiting for God to change her husband and marriage for 20 years. My life flashed before me. That wouldn't be me. "Please God, don't let that be me."

I started staying up at night once he'd fallen asleep and doing research on my computer downstairs. I had to figure out what was going on. I could feel myself being mentally unstable and I couldn't tell anymore if it was him who was dangerous, or me who was sick, or both. I somehow, by God's grace, came upon an expert who had been in a marriage for many years with an emotionally abusive spouse with a personality disorder. As he wrote about his life and the abuse that his ex-wife had used against him, I saw myself. God used this man to help save my life. I was then led to private chat rooms filled with women who were in abusive relationships with narcissists. They all said the same things: Their identities had been completely stripped away due to the constant hypervigilance of having to keep the narcissist's rage at bay. Many of these women had children and, along with stealing their identities, the narcissist had also created a situation in which the women were completely financially and emotionally dependent upon them

Living with a narcissist equals living in a continual state of fight, flight, or freeze. I felt like a detective. Every moment I had to myself when I was not with him, or teaching a class, I was looking online to find validation for the insanity I was experiencing. I found the DSM-5 diagnostic traits for narcissist and sociopath. It was him. I was sure of it. More terrifying than that was that I could not let him know that I knew, because I didn't know what he'd do to me if he knew. So I didn't fight. I also didn't flee, because I didn't have a plan yet. I did the only other thing I could do, given the circumstances: I froze.

I remember one Saturday afternoon bending over in front of the refrigerator. I could feel my lower back was exposed and he was behind me in the kitchen. The thought went through my mind that he was going to hit me. I stood there, completely vulnerable. I was petrified but I thought I cannot let him know that I know and, if he does this, I will have my evidence. He never hit me but I felt his eyes digging into me. I know that if he thought he could have got away with it, he would have. But he was biding his time.

I started losing more and more sleep. It got to the point where I was only sleeping one to two hours per night. This lasted for months. I went to the doctor and he put me on antidepressants, but that did not help my sleep. I was an anxious wreck. I would stay in bed as long as I could before having to go to the university, not being able to sleep, but also being too despondent to get out of bed. In between meetings and classes, I would lie on my office floor with the door closed and pray for the strength to get through the rest of the day. I was not present. My mind was continually replaying the last thing that he had said or did to me—searching for my evidence that he was dangerous and that I wasn't just making this all up. And I couldn't tell anyone.

I woke him up in the middle of the night many nights. I was filled with anxiety and I wanted answers. He seemed to be most truthful with me in the middle of the night because he was half-asleep and angry, and just wanted me to let him go back to sleep. I will never forget one night of fighting and me asking him why he was treating me this way and what I had done wrong to deserve this? He looked me straight into my eyes and, with the coldest stare I can imagine, he said these words: "Don't you get it, Melissa? I don't care about anyone else but myself." There it was. His confession. All of my research confirmed. I was right. He had no empathy nor ability to love. Every moment of happiness I had shared with him had all been pure manipulation. I was prey and he was the predator. And now that I was trapped he could tell me the truth. Not only did he not love me now, he had never loved me. He was incapable of love and empathy. I knew that I'd married a sociopath.

My appetite was completely gone. I lost 40 pounds. I couldn't sleep or eat. My entire system shut down. I would go home and pray I would get sleep. That's all I wanted and all I cared about. I became obsessed with it. None of the over-the-counter medications worked. The antidepressants didn't help at all. I would see his car pull up in the driveway and I would race for the bedroom, close the door, and get into bed. I thought that if I pretended I was asleep, he couldn't yell at me. I was living in an internal prison.

I was so incredibly stricken with panic that my body was causing me to throw up every morning, even though I hadn't been able to eat. I could only throw up water. My mind had already told my brain that there was something terribly wrong and now my body was breaking down in response. There was no more trying to escape the reality of my situation or pray that it would change. I could feel myself drowning.

I can recall standing in the bathroom one morning and looking at my reflection in the mirror. All of the light was gone from my eyes. The woman who stared back at me was vacant, a shell of who she had been. I did not recognize myself. I had no idea who this person was. My face was gaunt and my body was paralyzed by fear. So much fear I was ill. The thought of putting another anti-depressant capsule down my throat made me gag.

I went down to the dining room and there he was, finishing his breakfast and fixing his tie; I was wearing a pink bathrobe that was about ten years old. This was one of the most helpless moments I remember having with him. I could feel myself being desperately dependent upon the very person who had caused me to be sick. It was terrifying, but I felt like I had no one else to help me. I begged him not to go to work. I literally laid on the dining room floor and told him I couldn't do this anymore and pleaded with him to help me. I was in despair and felt myself dying, so I reached out to my mental and emotional murderer in one last effort with the hope that he might have a shred of empathy or even a tiny drop of love for me.

He yelled at me to get up off the floor, picked up the anti-depressant medication from the table, looked at me directly into my eyes, and said, "You should be careful with this. This medication can cause suicidal thoughts. Heaven forbid that should happen to you." I knew at that moment that this was a direct quote from Satan himself, trying to plant the thought in my mind to kill myself. I was convinced that my husband actually wanted me to die. He turned around, left the room, got into his car, and drove away. I laid back down on the floor in agony. I was powerless. There is no feeling I know that is worse than knowing you are mentally sick and knowing that there is nothing in your power to do anything about it and that the person who is supposed to love you caused your downfall. It is the feeling of pure helplessness, mixed with inescapable mental anguish and suffering.

Christmas break came and I was able to take some time away from my job at the university. I left the house and fled to my parent's home without telling him. I could not stay in that toxic house one more moment. I thank God I had a place to escape. I don't know what I would have done without my parent's support throughout this time in my life. I know many women who are in abusive relationships, who feel they have no place to go and no support. I was extremely fortunate.

Christmas Eve arrived. Our family tradition for years had been to go with Charlotte, my "inherited grandmother," as I call her, to her church in my hometown of Portland, Maine. I was so afraid to leave my parent's home and to see anyone that I almost didn't go. However, I forced myself to go because I wanted to see Charlotte, and I'm so very glad I did because it was her last Christmas Eve here with us before going home to our Heavenly Father. In the bathroom by myself at Trinity Church before the service, I pleaded with God: "God, if you will just save me from this, and take this sickness from me, I promise I will serve you for the rest of my life. Please, just save me from this mental anguish!" I begged him.

The Christmas Eve service that night was about the messiness of the miracle of the birth of Jesus. The reverend shared about how God chose to bring The Light of the World into the world in a smelly, dark stable through an unwed mother. Nothing about Jesus's arrival was neat and clean; it was a story filled with an unplanned pregnancy, rumors, isolation, long journeys, and difficult conditions, and yet this is how

God allowed it to occur. The reverend told us that if our lives looked messy and out of control, and if it seemed as if all hope was lost, this is exactly what the miracle of Jesus's birth and Christmas Eve was all about. I recall sitting in that pew and knowing at that moment that this was God's message directly for me on Christmas Eve 2014. I was in the mess and God was in the mess with me. I was not alone.

I found myself sitting in the office of a psychiatrist on New Year's Eve day. After we talked, I looked at him and told him I'd been hearing voices. And it was true. They were not audible and I knew that they were an attack of the enemy, but I also knew if I told the psychiatrist this, he would want me to voluntarily check myself into the psychiatric hospital. I had to do something. I was not getting any better on the anti-depressant medication and I still wasn't getting any sleep. Again, I was desperate. I thought maybe if I went to the hospital they could get me on the right medications and I could finally get some sleep. I could not think clearly, and I barely recall being able to fill out the paperwork. I was incredibly sick.

New Year's Eve was spent in a hospital bed in the emergency room waiting for a bed in the psychiatric hospital. It was a very long night. I would have never guessed six months before that this is where I would be spending my New Year's Eve. But nothing mattered to me anymore except getting some sleep and getting my mind back. I just wanted the perpetual mental torment to end. I needed the voices that continuously told me I was going to hell to stop.

I was transferred to the psychiatric hospital on New Year's Day. I spent the next two weeks in this hospital…the first two weeks of 2015. I can honestly say that those were the worst two weeks of my life. I still believed that God was angry at me, had cast me away, and would never forgive me for the mistakes I had made. I was convinced I was going to hell. I've never felt spiritual oppression as deeply as I did in that hospital. I was visited by a former pastor, and recovered addict, who sat with me in the private visitor's room at the table I confided in him that I felt the demonic surrounding me. He confirmed that the hospital was filled with demonic spirits. I was incredibly grateful to him at that moment because his experience of this spiritual sense confirmed that this wasn't just me going crazy. This place was plagued with souls being tormented.

I saw and felt many scary things in the hospital. People covered with the scars of self-harm. People who were disheveled and unclean. People talking to themselves and being held down against their will, given shots to medicate them into submission and sedation. I felt so out of place: me with all of my privilege, me with a doctoral degree. Here in this hospital. Having no control and power over my own life. I had never known what it was like to have absolutely no control over your own choices until then. When the door locks behind you on the unit, you know this is real. You are in their territory now.

They searched my bags and took away anything that I could use to hurt myself or someone else. They took away the tie to my bathrobe. I had to ask for my shampoo and conditioner when I took a shower. The water in the shower was cold and you had to continue to press the button throughout to get a continual stream of water. I still hadn't slept. This was made worse by the fact that the staff checks on you throughout the night every fifteen minutes: suicide watch. The light goes on, and there is no possibility of falling asleep. I realized that I was not going to get better in this place. There was a fleeting moment in the shower when I thought about what would happen if I drank my entire bottle of shampoo. I quickly rebuked the thought from my mind. It scared me that it even came into my mind. I couldn't see myself ever getting better. I thought, "I'm never going to get out of here. I'm never going to know freedom again. I'm going to be locked up in a hospital for the rest of my life. This is hopeless."

I pleaded with my psychiatrist to give me a higher dose of sleeping medication. I would pace back and forth every morning in front of the staff desk waiting for him to meet with me. I knew the power for me to sleep or not to sleep that night was resting in his hands putting the correct prescription and dose onto that pad of paper. He was young. I reasoned he was inexperienced as well. He seemed to do everything "by the book." I cared little for the rules at that point. I needed him to put me to sleep. The only feeling I experienced at that point was fear. No sadness. No tears. No depression. Just fear. I wouldn't wish this internal hell on anyone. It was the most isolating and petrifying experience of my life.

There was a particular room, kind of like a capsule, that was fully enclosed and padded on all sides with a small window. It was a kind of "panic room" reserved for hospital patients who were out of control and a danger to themselves and others. I was so desperate for sleep, that I actually began requesting every morning to sleep in this "panic room." I reasoned that at least I could be contained, and the 15-minute checks would be less intrusive. I hoped that I could even sleep for one hour within this capsule. Often the staff would not be able to give me an answer because they needed to wait to see if the space would have to be used for an emergency. I was able to sleep there a couple of nights; however, one of those nights was most likely one of the most vicious attacks of the enemy. The enemy tormented me throughout the night with ungodly acts and thoughts I had in my past. It was a continual reminder of my certain impending doom. I cannot express the deep sense of separation from God that I felt throughout those days and nights. I believed fully that He had abandoned me because of my sin. I was unable to express this deep spiritual torment to anyone else as I knew that they would only see it as a symptom of my mental instability. But internally, I was convinced that there was no hope for my soul.

After two weeks of not getting any better, I was sure the hospital was a lost cause at helping me. Then I had an idea. My mother, who has suffered from severe and chronic clinical depression for all of my adult life, has depended on electroconvulsive therapy (ECT) as the treatment that has worked to bring her from a catatonic state to functional. After her first hospitalization, the doctors labeled her as "medication-resistant," and suggested ECT. ECT is an outpatient treatment in which the patient is put to sleep and receives a mild electroconvulsive shock, resulting in a mild seizure to the brain. Think of it as a "jump start" for the brain. I reasoned to myself that if I explained my family history to the medical staff at the hospital, and told them that if they discharged me I would get ECT, they would let me go. I was right. They discharged me the next day, and I went home with the promise that I would participate in the hospital's intensive outpatient program (IOP), which met every day, and would also start ECT treatments.

That winter in Maine was one of the snowiest I remember. It seemed that we were pummeled with a blizzard every other day. My father brought me to the hospital every morning for the IOP. I would bring my lunch with me. Even though it was outpatient treatment, I still felt like I was imprisoned. Each morning would start with check-ins. There was a mixture of participants with mental health diagnoses, as well as co-occurring disorders (addiction and mental illness). I can recall sitting and listening to other participants discuss their long-standing disorders with alcohol, cocaine, and heroin addictions. I remember thinking to myself, "At least you can sleep." I am not kidding. I literally thought in those meetings that I would rather have an addiction like they had and be able to sleep than continue with my insomnia. It's not rational, I realize. But that is how greatly I needed sleep.

In the afternoons, we had lessons with Dan. He was charismatic and wore funny hats. He taught us about the illnesses of co-dependency and the havoc that living in the state of fight-or-flight wreaked on our central nervous systems, creating both physical and mental states of disease. His motto was "skills not pills." As much as I believed that I needed to learn healthy skills to cope with what I was going through, even more I needed a pill that would actually work to help put me to sleep. If I could just get one good night of sleep, I reasoned…I could start getting better.

Dan photocopied entire books for me to read and entire CD sets to listen to. He encouraged me not to isolate myself, (even though that's exactly what the depressed brain tells you to do) and to practice meditation and thought-stopping strategies. I thought of all of the times that I had told clients to practice skills and healthy coping strategies; and now I was too sick to do any of it myself. I would go into IOP with the same story every day: "I can't sleep. That's all I want. When can I meet with the psychiatrist?"

I remember a specific lesson that was taught about co-dependency and, at that moment, the teacher put words to what I'd known in my heart my entire life but tried to hide from others, from God, and most of all myself. I never felt secure within myself. I always looked to other people, things, or accomplishments to feel safe. I didn't really trust that God loved me and that I was secure in Him. I didn't do anything in my life unless I knew the outcome and knew I would be safe. And most of what I did, I did so I could figure out what the next safe step would be. The realization of this brought me to a place of dissociation. It was all I could do but keep from vomiting in the classroom. When you realize the depth of your own brokenness for the first time, it is nothing short of an out-of-body experience. But now I was starting to connect why I'd done what I'd done for so long. And I had no idea that recovery or healing was even an option. I was sure I would always be this broken.

I almost didn't go to ECT treatments. I was so afraid. My mother sat beside me as I wept in distress on the couch. "You would not have let *me* not go to this treatment," she told me. "You have to fight this, Melissa. You have to fight." Soon after, I arrived at the hospital for my first ECT treatment. My father and Nicole, my best friend since sixth grade, brought me. Except for my immediate family, Nicole is the only other person I trusted to see me in that condition. She's the safest person I know, and I trust her completely. I knew the doctors were going to put me under anesthesia and I was convinced I was going to die. I thought this was all part of the plan for my demise. I would die on this day at the hospital and go to hell. No one could tell me any different. I didn't share this delusion with anyone because I knew they would try to convince me otherwise. It took me over an hour to give them permission to start the IV. I was more than panicked.

I'm not sure what finally made me give in. Maybe it was Nicole, standing there so patiently. Maybe it was a belief that, if I was going to have to continue to live this way, I might as well just let go. Or maybe there was still someplace hidden deep within my spirit that wanted to believe that this very last option could actually save my life. So they started the IV, brought me into the small treatment room with the large electric machine, hooked electrodes onto several places on my head, and told me to breathe deeply as they placed the mask over my face. Immediately, I began to feel the anesthesia go into my veins and, for the first time in almost six months, I felt the fear leave my body and mind. I woke up crying. I was alive.

It would be at least two weeks of treatments before the depression began to lift. Thinking of this moment still brings tears to my eyes. It had become our tradition to go out to breakfast at "Our Place," as we called it, on the way home from treatments, because I could not eat anything in the morning before going to the hospital. That's when it happened. I'm not sure who it was, my father or Nicole, but someone said something that made me laugh. It happened naturally, without me thinking about it. I didn't even see it coming. I looked up at Nicole's eyes, filled with tears, looking back at me. "You just laughed," she said. "You're coming back."

I will be forever grateful for that moment. I will be forever grateful to my father, my mother, my sister, my niece, my best friend, all of my friends, my ECT doctors, the team of nurses and CNAs, and every person who believed in my life and future when I had given up all hope. I will be forever grateful to God. If you are reading this now, you must know this truth: You are never too far out of God's reach for Him to pull you out from the depths of despair you are in. I am living proof. Miracles still happen.

4

Under The Shadow Of The Almighty: Resting In The Shelter Of God

Whoever dwells in the shelter of the Most High
will rest in the shadow of the Almighty.
I will say of the LORD, "He is my refuge and my fortress,
My God, in whom I trust."

~ Psalms 91:1-2

I spent the next two months living at my parent's home in the midst of a Maine winter, spending a lot of time in an 8 x 8 bedroom. I learned to rest in that bedroom. I moved everything I owned into a storage unit and the life I had thought

I was going to live was wiped clear away. I was on medical leave from my teaching job for the semester and there was nothing to do but heal. I found God's shelter in that back bedroom. I spent every morning looking out the window at the snow-covered backyard and noticing the birds come to the bird feeder. It was as if God was whispering to me, "If I take care of them, I'll take care of you. If I can provide for them in the depths of the darkness of winter, I can heal you."

I started a ritual in that bedroom of getting up early, going to get my morning coffee, and going back to my bed to read my Bible. I found peace reading for hours and meditating on what God was speaking to me through His Word. In a situation where it had seemed as if I had lost everything and all was uncertain, God showed me that He would not forsake me. I spent hours, days, and weeks, crying over my rescue.

God was using the darkest season of my life to reconcile me to Himself. He used my time in isolation with Him to restore my relationship with Him. He was demonstrating to me in real time, when I felt the most helpless and unworthy, the truth and the comfort of His Word:

Therefore, if anyone is in Christ, the new creation has come.
The old has gone, the new is here!
All this is from God, who reconciled us to himself
through Christ
And gave us the ministry of reconciliation:

That God was reconciling the world to himself in Christ,
Not counting people's sins against them.
And he has committed to us the message of reconciliation.

2 Corinthians 5:17-19

I prayed and rested; and rested and prayed. I read and meditated on my Bible like never before. It became so refreshing that I looked forward to my time in that small bedroom every morning. I depended on it as I depended on my very breath. It was my peace and security. The time alone with God in that tiny room brought me back to life.

I had entered the realm of the *Secret Place*. I learned to listen to the *still small voice*. I had nothing else I could do, and nowhere else I could go, but into *His presence*. I started to recognize it as a gift, this time away from the world. Nothing was expected of me. I had no obligations and no responsibilities to tend to daily. My greatest priority and focus was to allow God to heal me.

I had to learn to humble myself in the process and let God take His time. My healing was not dependent on me. There was nothing I could do. I was powerless to heal myself of the deep psychological, emotional, and spiritual trauma I had experienced. Only God Himself could do this. I had to let go of all control and go through the process of healing that he had already planned for me. I had to learn to trust Him.

I prayed that God would not only fully restore me, but that He would pay me back ten-fold for everything the enemy had stolen from me. I prayed that every moment of suffering I had been through and was going through would not be in vain and that God would use it all, through me, to help others. I knew even then that I was far from being the only woman in this position and in my Spirit, I envisioned the many women God would help through me once I was healed.

I had a small throw rug on the floor of the bedroom at the foot of my bed. This rug became my alter. It was so small and sheltered in that room that I felt safe enough to breathe again. It was confined and narrow enough that I felt protected. Kneeling on that rug, with my face on the floor, became my daily practice. I experienced Psalms 139:5 on my knees on that piece of woven fabric: *You hem me in behind and before, and you lay your hand upon me.*

One of the most powerful moments I've ever had with Jesus was kneeling, face down, on that rug. I was crying out to God in my pain and heartbreak. I had come to the recognition that the man I had married was truly a sociopath and not only lacked conscience about the evil he had committed against me but was truly unable to even feel empathy. The pain of this revelation struck a chord so deeply within me and the trauma of this truth ran through my entire body. I cannot tell you why this was so greatly heartbreaking to me, other than just to say that this person, whom I had given myself to, shattered my heart, mind, and spirit into a million pieces, and I *knew* he would never even have the capacity to understand the overwhelming pain that he had caused me. It was the greatest sense of betrayal I've ever experienced.

It was in this moment of profound sorrow that Jesus reached out to me. In my spirit, I saw a picture of Jesus hanging on the cross, being betrayed, ridiculed, killed; and they did not know what they had done. My God had experienced this exact feeling, and far, far worse than I would ever know. I saw myself in the emotional pain and isolation I was experiencing hanging with Jesus on the other side of that cross. There was *nothing* separating us. We were truly ONE. I have never felt so close to Jesus than at that very moment. I will never forget that gift of intimacy as long as I live.

He reminded me of His words on the cross, "Forgive them, Father, for they know not what they do." Through tears, agony, and crying out to God, I let go at that moment. I asked God to give me the grace to forgive my perpetrator. God gave me the grace to forgive the person who had caused such devastation in my life, who would never know the depths of pain he had caused me, and who would never ask for my forgiveness. I prayed that day that God would make a way to save his soul, and I began the process of releasing him.

During this time in the secret place, God began to show me that my suffering was not in vain. I had been consumed with feelings of shame, guilt, and humiliation. I had a PhD in the field of clinical mental health counseling. How could I have allowed myself to marry a sociopath? How could I have become so desperately depressed? How could I not help myself? I wondered at times if my entire career would be over. Would anyone trust the integrity of my professional reputation ever again?

Then it occurred to me that the best healers are those who have had to fight for their own healing. The best people to hold someone up in the midst of deep pain and suffering are the ones who know what it's like to suffer deeply. From this moment on, I would be able to relate to every student, client, and person I met with greater empathy and compassion than ever before. And it wouldn't be because I read about the conditions of psychological abuse, insomnia, panic attacks, anxiety, severe clinical depression, and PTSD through books; it would be because I myself had lived through them.

Looking back on this time of recovery, I learned something foundational about God: He loves us so greatly that He will not only take our shining moments of success and accomplishments to propel us forward and to bring Himself glory; He will also take our greatest mistakes and failures, our sicknesses, our sorrows, our grief; and He will work it all together for our good, and His purpose. He will take what we thought we'd never recover from, what we thought we had broken beyond repair, and use it to help and heal someone else. I've seen it with my own eyes. And if you are reading this book, He's doing it right now.

There were times early on that I was still afraid to drive on my own, to go to appointments on my own, or to walk downtown on my own. I had to re-learn how to feel safe. My body and mind had to gradually shift from living in fight-or-flight to homeostasis again. I had to find my internal balance again.

I distinctly recall going to my psychiatrist appointment one afternoon and being afraid to walk down the street to my car by myself. The appointment was only about a twenty-minute drive from my home and the walk to the car was about five minutes. A part of my brain—the rational part, told me I was okay, and I would make it safely. My body told me a different story. Trauma is stored in the brain and the body. It took years to work through what had happened to me, and what led up to my trauma. It was not an overnight fix. But God is good, and His faithfulness endures forever.

I continued to go to ECT treatments. At first, I went to the hospital twice a week and gradually I went once a week. After time, it was every other week and slowly the treatments lessened as I began to sleep again and function. I attended weekly counseling sessions to support my continued journey of healing. I gradually started seeing friends in social settings. Since driving is prohibited during times of intensive ECT treatments, my sister often invited me and brought me to social events with her. Every friend was gracious to me. My judgment of myself was far worse than from anyone else...at least that I knew of!

The understanding that trauma was trapped in my body registered in a serious way when I began attending restorative yoga classes. Restorative yoga is made up of a series of deep stretches that are done slowly and deliberately to allow both the body and mind to relax and rest. Often there are only five or six poses that are done in an hour-long class. As I went through the poses in this weekly or sometimes twice-weekly class, I would often be brought to the point of weeping.

Releasing my physical self was allowing something to be released in my psychological/emotional/spiritual self. I would allow myself to cry, knowing that no one in that room would judge me. I could rest in those classes, knowing I was surrounded by safe people. I was able to let go and begin to feel safe again on the yoga mat. Going to those classes was one of the gifts of healing. There is no doubt in my mind that the practice of yoga is helpful to bring integration and healing back to the body and the mind.

Slowly, my mind, body, and soul began to heal. I began to reach out to friends more. I let people know that I was making my way back to life. When I reached my 37th birthday, on March 30th, I was out to dinner looking down a long table at the beautiful faces of a large group of friends. This was the first night I had got my hair done, got dressed up, put on makeup, and gone out past 7 o'clock in months. I felt like it was my entrance back into the land of the living. That birthday was more than celebrating my birthday. I was celebrating being brought back to life.

That summer, I went back to teaching three online classes at the university to ease myself back into work. Each student welcomed me back with open arms. I was amazed at the amount of love and care that poured over me from those who had been concerned about my well-being in my absence. Not only did I have dear family and friends supporting me during my darkest season, but I also had students and colleagues sending me cards, thoughts, and prayers when I was on leave. I realized during this time how very much I was loved by others and how much my personal welfare mattered to those who loved me. It was humbling to realize that people I didn't even know had been praying for me.

In August, on the one-year anniversary of the day I had got married, I asked my parents if they would go to the lake with me. It was a beautiful sunny day in Maine at one of my favorite places with amazing childhood memories. The clear water at Sebago Lake State Park was gleaming under the blue skies and summer sun. I have a photo of myself with my parents. My smile is large, and I am glowing with joy. Gratitude filled my eyes. I know I cried later that day in my bedroom alone, but the tears were a combination of thanksgiving and release. I thanked God for rescuing me from the pit of despair, for restoring my mental and physical health, and for giving me another chance at life. Several days later, I was divorced. He had finally realized he was never going to get me back, so he gave up the power struggle and control, stopped fighting it, and let me go. This season of my life was coming to an end. God was in the process of mending my wounds and I still have the scars to show you.

5

Reactive Attachment Disorder With God: Old Patterns Die Hard

Therefore, I tell you, her many sins have been forgiven—
as her great love has shown.
But whoever has been forgiven little loves little.

~ Luke 7:47

Have you ever been so ashamed of something that you didn't think you'd ever be forgiven? Have you ever been so utterly lost and broken that you thought you'd never find your way home to God, or even to your own self? Have you ever looked at your life and dysfunctional behaviors and thought,

"I don't even know where or how to begin to find my way out of this"? Have you ever wondered if you'd ever *truly* be free? These questions are what this chapter is all about. One might think that, after everything I had already been through, I was healed. Not so fast. I had been through terror and been rescued. However, I didn't realize at the time that I had yet to get to the roots of my problems and my healing journey was just beginning.

One day before I was due to move into my own apartment, I saw his picture on the Animal Refuge League's website. He was an eight-week-old puppy named Sherman and he had the cutest face I'd ever seen. I had been receiving emails for weeks but hadn't found the right puppy until that moment. My niece, Corinna, texted me that I had to be the first one there to assure that I had first choice. She told me, "Don't shower. Just get dressed." So I jumped out of bed, put on some clothes, and we immediately went to adopt him that morning. Corinna was right. We were there first and we got him! My relationship with my niece is one of my life's greatest blessings and she made sure I got another one of my greatest blessings: Sherman.

I had always wanted a dog and adopting Sherman was one of the best decisions I've ever made. He has been my companion, and best friend, ever since. We moved into our new apartment together a day later. I recall looking down at him eating a piece of cardboard from the corner of the box of dishes on the kitchen floor and saying to him, "Okay, it's you and me. Let's figure this out together." I was brand-new to him, he was brand-new to me, and this apartment was brand-new to both of us. He trusted me to take care of him and I trusted him to love me unconditionally. I believe that God gave me Sherman to teach me how to love again and how to feel safe again. We started this new life together.

I unpacked my boxes, set up my apartment, and went back to work at the university full time. It was my first actual time living on my own with a full-time job, and not being a "professional student." There was a lot to learn. At first, I was focused on my work and on Sherman. I was busy keeping up my apartment, performing the daily tasks of life, and getting to know neighbors. But too much freedom with no accountability is disastrous.

Once I was off of my anti-depressant medication, on which I had not consumed alcohol for about a year and a half, I began enjoying an occasional glass of wine again. The trouble was, for me that an occasional glass became a glass every night, which became two glasses, which became a half bottle of wine a night. It was too easy for me to have a glass when I came home from work, a glass when I made dinner, and a glass after dinner. What I didn't realize at the time was that the wine for me was a counterfeit for community and an imitation of connection. Instead of connecting to God, others, and myself, wine was a way to disconnect from the stresses of the day. I used it as a coping mechanism and as an escape.

Due to using wine in this way, and also eating all the food I wanted and cooked for myself (this girl loves to cook!), I gained about 20 pounds. The weight went on slowly but surely. I started to not be able to fit into the professional clothes that I once wore and traded in my tailored pants for leggings. I continued to drink and eat, not realizing that I was actually self-medicating feelings, such as anxiety, sadness, regret, disappointment, and loneliness. The same old pattern of abusing food and alcohol was resurfacing.

My waistline was not the only thing expanding. I started to take a better look at my credit card debt and noticed it continued to skyrocket month to month. I was not keeping a budget and was clearly not making enough money to support my expenses. I was drowning in debt between credit cards, car loan, and college loans, and I did not have the first idea of how to deal with these issues. I continued to put bills and items on my credit card that I couldn't afford to pay in any other way. I had no idea how I would break free of this downward spiral.

Finally, there was the pattern of online dating. Whenever I felt lonely, putting a dating application back on my phone was my answer. I longed for connection but still did not know where or how to find it in a healthy way. There was also a part of me that longed for validation and affirmation from men, especially for my outward appearance. I still believed that the only way to earn attention and love from a man was through my physical self. I wanted to feel desired, but this was just an illusion. Deep down, I really just wanted to be loved, but I didn't yet know what love truly is and I also didn't think I was worthy of healthy love.

Many of these online "situationships" ended up being simply lots of text conversations with little depth or substance. Some involved "sexting." Some led to a date. Some led only to a "hookup." The deception I was under at the time as a single grown woman was that this was my choice to date and to have sex with men. I rationalized and justified my behaviors and used alcohol as a way to shut off the conviction of the Holy Spirit. However, none of this was done with keeping my emotional, psychological, spiritual, and physical safety and self-worth intact. Often, I was under the influence of alcohol, just as I had been in past seasons.

Being intoxicated shuts down one's discernment, inhibitions, and conscience. For me, drinking alcohol and having sex with men has always been a form of self-harm and spiritual suicide disguised as self-gratification. The truth is, no relationship ever developed. The men never called afterward. They didn't actually care about me, much less love me, and I always felt guilty and condemned the next day. This pattern of behavior only grew my sense of shame and unworthiness, my lack of secure identity and lack of attachment to myself and God, and feelings of being dirty and hopeless at my core. It was a cycle I thought I would never escape.

The enemy knew that the sin that so easily entangled me would be the sin that would cause me the most shame. He knew that the sin against my very body would keep me in bondage not only in my own guilt and shame but would keep me in the cycle of hiding from and being distanced from God.

Flee from sexual immorality. All other sins a person commits are outside the body, but whoever sins sexually, sins against their own body.

1 Corinthians 6:18

This sin against my own body in the form of alcohol abuse and sexual promiscuity would keep me believing the lie that I would never be worthy of true love: from myself, from a man, or, most devastatingly, from God.

REACTIVE ATTACHMENT DISORDER WITH GOD

The diagnosis of reactive attachment disorder in children, as defined by the American Psychiatric Association's *Diagnostic and Statistical Manual of Mental Disorders*, Fifth Edition, [DSM-5, 313.89 (F94.10)], includes the following as *one* of the criteria for diagnosis: "A consistent pattern of inhibited, emotionally withdrawn behavior toward adult caregivers, manifested by both of the following: 1. The child rarely or minimally seeks comfort when distressed. 2. The child rarely or minimally responds to comfort when distressed." Again, this is just one of the criteria for RAD in children, a diagnosis that is rooted in the child having experienced neglect and abuse.

Although I did not experience neglect and abuse as a child, I experienced rejection from others and from myself, and this damaged my perception of myself and my self-worth. I began to realize that, much like a traumatized child, I reacted by pushing my Heavenly Father away, and attempted instead to rely upon my own failed attempts at self-soothing, instead of running into His loving arms. Because I did not fully believe that I was worthy of love or that God would actually desire to comfort me after all of my failures, I continued to run after all other forms of consolation I could find on my own, instead of running to Him. I was afraid of fully surrendering and trusting God to care for me, so I pushed Him away, and tried to care for myself.

So there I was: a 38-year-old woman with a job teaching at a university, with a beautiful apartment in a Victorian home. Everything on the outside seemed to be in place, but I knew that everything on the inside was an absolute mess. I was tired of being one person on the outside and a totally different person on the inside. The incongruence between who I was proposing to be on the outside and how I was living behind closed doors was becoming unbearable. I was still hiding from God on the inside, and I knew it.

The roots of rejection and unworthiness of the experiences of my past had caused my little broken girl on the inside to believe that she had to continue to go around to the back entrance in secret, in an attempt to get my adult needs met. Instead of coming up to the palace doors with my head held high, as a Child of God, I was still behaving as if I was an illegitimate child. I didn't know my full identity in Christ yet; therefore, I was living a life where I was trying to get my emotional needs met by myself and in all of the wrong ways.

You can understand that the broken little girl inside of the woman is still trying to take responsibility for meeting your adult needs when you continue to find yourself going after the "shiny object" that you feel will give you gratification, validation, identity, affirmation, and love. The shiny object might be in the form of abusing food and substances, participating in promiscuous relationships, or gratifying yourself by buying things you can't afford. And you can be sure that I've tried all of these.

Remember: The snake in the garden was shining. "Serpent" can be translated into "shining one." Satan was an angel of light. *Now the serpent was more crafty than any of the wild animals the LORD God had made. He said to the woman, "Did God really say, 'You must not eat from any tree in the garden'?" (Genesis 3:1)*. Satan is the father of lies. In fact, another name for the enemy is "morning star" or "shining one." Lucifer's body was a beautiful shining instrument created to glorify the Lord. Instead of using what God had given him for glorying God, he distorted God's plan to glorify Himself. This distortion of our physical bodies to glorify ourselves instead of God is an echo of Lucifer's fall and a product of our fallen nature. It's part of the enemy's plan to hold us captive and in bondage to sexual sin.

How you have fallen from heaven
Morning star, son of the dawn!
You have been cast down to the earth,
You who once laid low the nations!
You said in your heart,
"I will ascend to the heavens;
I will raise my throne
above the stars of God;
I will sit enthroned on the mount of assembly,
on the utmost heights of Mount Zaphon.
I will ascend above the tops of the clouds;
I will make myself like the Most High."

Isaiah 14:12-14

Just like Lucifer's original fall from grace due to pride, my sexual sin was a form of pride, self-reliance, and distortion. I attempted to glorify myself and meet my own needs, acting in disobedience to God. All the while, my shame grew deeper. Even if I "acted out" sporadically, it was a cycle that I felt I could never break and I could never be made fully clean. Not only did I experience shame and separation from God due to this cycle, but also extreme psychological pain caused by knowing that I was allowing men who didn't love me to use me. I was so desperate for love that I allowed myself to be hurt in this way and this reality caused me a level of spiritual, emotional, and psychological pain that became unendurable. I knew I was hurting myself by engaging in these behaviors. This is why 1 Corinthians 6:18 says, "Flee from sexual immorality. All other sins a person commits are outside the body, but whoever sins sexually, sins against their own body."

I continued to go backward to new lovers and past boyfriends, reigniting emotional and sometimes sexual bonds in an attempt to feel safe and gain a stable sense of identity, but this never worked because our true identity is in Christ alone. Would you believe me if I told you that God actually used one of the men that I had sex with to tell me, "You don't really want sex. You are looking for something else"? God was allowing this man to tell me the truth about myself. What I really wanted was emotional intimacy, and even *this* man could tell! The truth is that I was terrified of true intimacy for fear of rejection, even though I longed for it.

I was stuck in a continuous cycle of unworthiness, shame, guilt, performance, and striving. I lacked a sense of belonging in the Body of Christ due to my fear of rejection, and inner shame. This lack of belonging led to further self-isolation, as well as a lack of understanding of my true value and significance that can only be found in intimate emotional giving and receiving in safe communities. I went through cycles of hiding from true intimacy with others, and even hiding from the love of God. I engaged in behavioral patterns of rejecting myself, harming myself, betraying myself, and abandoning myself. I have come to learn that, although I was saved and believed in Jesus, I still carried an orphan spirit, instead of the spirit of a Child of God. These were all symptoms of my identity crisis! I did not yet grasp my identity in Christ, and, because of this, I was trapped in these harmful cycles.

I have come to learn that whatever you struggle with most is what God is going to break off of you to release the fullness of your anointing. If your struggle is with pride, fear of man, perfectionism, striving, performance, and a spirit of self-reliance, like mine is, guess what God is going to do? He is going to cause you to be vulnerable and humble and bring you to a place where you cannot depend upon yourself. God is going to do this because He knows when you die to yourself where your *self* most struggles, He'll only then be able to release the *Fullness of Himself.* I've also come to learn how painful this journey is and how very much this process of healing hurts. But it is for our good and for His glory!

Years before this stage in my life, I had a dream. In the dream, there was a huge field. There, in the middle of the field, was a beautiful, single, red rose. In the dream, I asked God what I would have to do to earn the rose. It has taken me years to understand that the dream wasn't about me needing to strive to achieve the rose. The dream was about God telling me that to Him, I am the rose. The rose represents His love for me, and how He sees me.

As I was walking on the beach one winter afternoon with Sherman running ahead of me, God clearly spoke to me in my heartache: "Melissa, if you would just finally run to Me the way you have run after everything else in this world in an attempt to comfort yourself, I would rescue you." It wasn't long thereafter that I found myself face down on the floor, weeping in my home office. Although I could barely gasp out the words, I know God heard my cries. I told Him how afraid I was. I told Him how I couldn't keep trying to do this on my own anymore because my life was a mess. I told him I was giving up control. I begged Him not to cast me aside, but to please take control of my life. I spent hours crying on the floor that day. I surrendered and released control to God over and over.

I tried to hold on, but every tear that fell softened my heart to let go. I told God I did not know how to have a healthy relationship with a man. He would have to teach me. Not only that, but I did not know how to have a healthy relationship with myself. And then the foundational confession: "God, I don't know how to have a healthy relationship with *YOU*. Please teach me. Please help me. Please heal me. You have to do this. I can't keep living in these cycles any longer. I give you control of my life."

And then, when I was finally quiet, God whispered this in my spirit, "Today, you are done searching for love. You are done trying to piecemeal love together." That day when I finally surrendered control of the mess I had made running after everything and everyone but God, was the day God ended my life-long search for love. He was about to show me that the love of my life was Him all along. The steel box I had constructed around my heart would shatter under the weight of His love. There are no walls that we can build up around ourselves that His love will not tear down.

6

My Broken Heart In The Hands Of Jesus: My Weakness And His Perfection

You do not delight in sacrifice or I would bring it;
you do not take pleasure in burnt offerings.
My sacrifice, O God, is a broken spirit; a broken and
contrite heart you, God, will not despise.

~ Psalms 50:16-17

Last winter I began to fall into another depressive episode. It always begins the same: first doubt sets in, then anxiety, then the impending doom that I won't have enough of what I need, (resources, security, support, or strength), to make it through. The doubt and anxiety merge into fear. Next comes sleeplessness. The world around me begins to feel as though it's closing in. The dull ache permeates throughout my body. My shoulders and back feel tender and weak and a cloud of darkness casts a shadow over my mind. The experience of internal isolation feels impenetrable. Clinical depression feels like trying to breathe underwater. It is an experience of being enveloped under a pressure that feels so dark, deep, and heavy, that even breathing feels like a strain. Depression brings with it physical and mental exhaustion so pervasive that the only thing you want to do is lie in bed but, even then, your mind won't let you rest. Your soul is tormented. The symptoms of depression are mental, physical, and spiritual.

One morning, I was kneeling before my bed and God gave me a vision of myself inside a prison cell. He told me that the door was unlocked. All I had to do was to get up, open the door, and walk out. He told me that I was in a prison of my own making. I realized that I had let anxiety and fear about finances overwhelm me. I had recently started my own business and, having left teaching at the university, it was my first winter trying to make ends meet exclusively on the income from my business. God was assuring me that He would provide, but I continued to struggle with unbelief and a scarcity mindset. I worried so much that I had made myself sick. It is exactly as James 1:6-7 says: "But when you ask, you must believe and not doubt, because the one who doubts is like a wave of the sea, blown and tossed by the wind. That person should not expect to receive anything from the Lord."

What I did not understand at the time about anxiety and depression, the Holy Spirit has since made clear to me. The enemy is the father of lies and he is a deceiver. He wants us to focus on the obvious, which would be him stealing our joy, but it is actually anxiety (which leads to fear) that is the precursor to depression. Depression is the impression that fear and anxiety leave behind.

1 Peter 5:8 tells us, "Be alert and of sober mind. Your enemy the devil prowls around like a roaring lion looking for someone to devour." The verse just before this says: "Cast all your anxiety on him because he cares for you." 1 Peter 5:7. The enemy knows that if he can steal your peace and your calm, your joy will come soon thereafter! Therefore, he doesn't go directly for your joy; he goes for your peace and your calm. He knows that if he can keep you in a place of anxiety and fear, depression will follow soon after. The enemy also knows that once you are depressed, you feel weak and hopeless, because "The joy of the Lord is your strength" (Nehemiah 8:10). Jesus says, "Therefore, I tell you, do not worry about your life" (Matthew 6:25). We often focus so greatly on God's external commandments, but I cannot think of an internal commandment from the Lord that I have more often broken than this one.

Don't let the enemy fool you! Joy is the daughter of Peace and Calm. This is the Perfect Peace of God despite our circumstances. I have since learned to protect my peace and calm at all costs, and realized only then that joy is the natural outcome of maintaining my Peace. Jesus Himself is the Prince of Peace and gives us perfect peace because we trust in Him. "Peace I leave with you; my peace I give you. I do not give to you as the world gives. Do not let your hearts be troubled and do not be afraid" (John 14:27).

Therefore, anything or anyone else that we try to set our security upon, other than God Himself, is a counterfeit. "Above all else, guard your heart, for everything you do flows from it" (Proverbs 4:23). Your heart is your mind. This is different than your physical brain. Your brain responds to your mind, not the other way around. Your mind is your very consciousness. Guarding your peace in your heart (the peace in the consciousness of your mind) is more important than anything else.

This past winter when I was struggling, I did all I could to get through the day and at night I would take a hot shower and lie on the bathroom mat, crying out to God. I called out for Abba. Please rescue me from this. Please don't let me fall so deep into this pit that I cannot get out. Some nights all I could do was lie on the mat and say His name over and over through tears. "Abba…Abba…Abba…please free me." I could feel all the while this time that something was different. Even in the midst of this darkness, I knew in my heart that this was occurring to free me. Every step I had walked in pain had been necessary for my deliverance.

One night during the darkness of winter, I was walking Sherman in the nearby woods and I collapsed to my knees in the snow. I could not hold the weight of the sorrow, grief, and pain inside my heart any longer. I pleaded with God to save me from this depression and to make me secure in Him and Him alone. I knew there were parts of myself inside that were still broken and I pleaded with him to take all of the internal mess I was carrying and to bring healing. Through a tear-drenched, frosted face, I surrendered control once again in desperation. I told God that He had to take my heart, in all of its broken pieces. I asked him to take all the parts I'd been too ashamed to show Him, and all of the parts I had tried to hide from Him, and to somehow make something beautiful, because only He could do this.

As I neared the front of my home, I stopped and placed my hands over my heart. I whispered a silent prayer to Jesus for my despondent heart, so heavy in my chest that every breath I took was a struggle. I could see my breath in a cloud in front of me in the cold, still, silent night air, and Jesus's words came back to me quickly in my Spirit: "I'm holding your heart. Your heart *is my very heart.*" Warm tears streamed down my face. At that moment I felt Jesus closer than my own breath. I saw my heart in His hands.

God will let your heart break from the things from your past that you've spent your whole life trying to repair. It will feel like your heart is breaking and healing, all at the same time. He'll do this not just to heal your heart, but to give you a brand-new heart. You're going to be okay, I promise. Just surrender. Let your heart break in his stable hands. Let Him do this. This is *His* process. He's going to make something beautiful—more beautiful than you could ever imagine.

It was in this place that I began to recognize that my experience of depression was also connected to my past trauma. I had become depressed every winter since my first major clinical depression and I started to understand that every winter I began to have a trauma response. I was not just troubled by the symptoms of depression, I was terrified of getting sick again beyond my level to find my way out and this fear would act as a catapult into deeper depression. Having gone through a deep clinical depression is in itself traumatizing. This trauma response continued to plague me winter after winter.

Secondly, I began to have the insight that my symptoms of depression were connected to my experience of insecure attachment. When I felt alone and isolated, I experienced a feeling of dissociation from myself, God, and others, and this experience was terrifying. Finally, I recognized that depression was a spiritual attack. There was a stronghold in my life that was demonic and it needed to be broken off.

Amid this darkness, I attempted to find help. I called my pastor and asked if there was anyone at my church that did deliverance ministry. I attended a two-hour inner healing session with experts at my church and many strongholds were broken off of my life that evening. God gave me truth after truth to replace the lies I had been believing. Most foundational to these truths whispered in my Spirit was who I am as a Daughter of the King. God told me that my identity as His daughter is: Loving, Honoring, Trusting, Whole, Secure, Safe, and Confident. This is who I really am.

I refer back to these words that God gave me to describe my identity in Him often. God also told me that evening that I would never again look to anyone else to fulfill me but to Him, because my adequacy comes from Him alone. It was during this time of deep healing that God replaced the lies that I would never have enough, or be enough, with the truths that I would always have enough, and I would always be enough because I belong to Him.

Along with the referral for inner healing ministry, my pastor had also given me the wisdom that I should spend time in intimacy with the Lord. He told me that I had nothing to be afraid of because I am God's. I recognized that the pattern of continuing to search for security in others had to come to an end. I cried out to God as I lay prostrate on my living room floor to heal this deep insecurity in my soul. I told God that I had to become completely secure in Him. Nothing short of utter security in Him would be enough!

The Lord answered me immediately with this simple statement: "You need to learn how to *rest* in Me." He told me to make this a practice. He went on to say in my spirit: "The more you learn how to rest in Me, the more securely attached you will become to Me. I am the foundation of all healthy attachment. I am your firm place to stand." It was like fireworks going off in my brain! It was the answer I had been searching for my entire life. God Himself was the answer to all of my attachment trauma and mental anguish. All security comes from God Himself and He was about to transform me from insecure to secure. He continued to speak: "Make Me your number one attachment. I will make you whole through time spent with Me because I AM WHOLENESS."

God spoke these set of instructions to me for my healing and transformation:

1. "Rest in Me, moment by moment. You *must* rest in Me."

2. "Do these things often: Have intimacy with Me, speak with Me, think on Me, reflect on Me, read My Word. These are the activities that bring you into a state of REST. It's Divine Rest. Not like the world gives, do I give."

3. "You will no longer be a Martha. You are becoming a Mary."

4. "Spend time in My Presence, ABOVE ALL THINGS."

The very next day, I prayed this prayer: "Lord, I surrender my will to Your will. I cast out all wills that do not align with Your perfect will for me. I know Your will is perfect, and the best for me. I want Your perfect will playing out in my life." Then I asked God this question: "What is Your will for me?" The answer God gave me was a vision of a bird flying freely overhead and the words, "Freedom in mind, heart, and spirit." I spoke out loud, "I claim Your will for me, Lord, of freedom of mind, heart, and spirit."

The very next day, I opened up my Bible to Psalms 124:7: "We have escaped like a bird from the fowler's snare; the snare has been broken, and we have escaped." I did not yet feel the symptoms of depression lift, but I knew in my Spirit that God had already given me the victory. I recognized this vision and verse as prophetic and I began to speak to the spirit of depression that I was victorious over it in Christ; I believed it and I commanded it to go in the name of Jesus.

Within several days thereafter, I joined a "Break the Cycle" online challenge and I claimed victory in the Blood of Jesus over a poverty/scarcity mindset, fear, depression, anxiety, and insomnia. I could physically feel the demonic spirits flee as I cast these spirits out and commanded them to go. I proclaimed that I am a child of The Most High God and cast these spirits into hell. I proclaimed that I am free! That very night, spiritual warfare came against me as nightmares in my sleep. I had to get up the next morning and rebuke the evil spirits attached to my sleep and my dream life as well. The process throughout this night of breaking these cycles was true warfare. I could feel the spirits fighting back but I clung to the Blood of Jesus as my protection and uprooted every evil spirit with the power of the Blood! No weapon formed against me shall prosper, or be able to stand against the King of Kings and Lord of Lords!

Let me tell you one more way that God answered my prayers last winter and then confirmed that it was Him and Him alone, who provided for all of my needs. I went to Roots Café, a Christian establishment near my home, and saw an audiobook on the shelf called *The Shelter of God's Promises* by Sheila Walsh. The title and the cover of the audiobook stood out to me immediately, with a woman standing beneath a bright red umbrella. I was able to borrow it from the lending library and began listening to the book right away. Listening to Sheila's beautiful voice with her tender Scottish accent read to me about God's promises and how it is His strength that is made perfect in my weakness was a healing balm for my broken heart and reeling mind. Her recounting of the story of Peter denying Christ and then Peter being the first and only disciple that Christ called by name when he was resurrected brought me to a place of weeping for over an hour in my car in the pouring rain. As Sheila said, it was when Peter had nothing to bring to the table—no gifts, no talents—just brokenness, this was when God was most glorified because He got to have what He was after all along— Peter's heart. It was at that moment last winter, in my car in the pouring rain, that I finally gave Jesus my whole heart with *ALL* the broken pieces.

I had no idea when listening to the book that Sheila had also struggled with the despair and hopelessness of clinical depression. Her truthful telling of her story helped free me. I also had no idea that, when I was going to come to the American Association of Christian Counselors World Conference this past October, Sheila would be a keynote speaker. As I sat in the audience of thousands and heard her voice, it clicked for me that *this* was the woman I had spent a month listening to this past winter. I could barely keep from bursting into inconsolable tears and falling onto my knees as this realization hit me. God had brought Sheila Walsh to this conference *just for me.* He was telling me that He had been there for *every single moment.* I was safe. I was safe. I was safe. The understanding of this truth nearly knocked me over. God was telling me *He sees me, He's with me, and I am safe.* I've never in my life had such a powerful moment of recognizing the lengths God will go to in order to show us that He sees us, and is with us. He is Immanuel. God with us.

Sheila's voice recounting the truth of God's promises had got me through some of my deepest moments of despair and led me to healing. And then I realized that God had not only brought her book to me as a minister of His healing but had brought me face to face with her eight months later. I got to walk up to her, look into her eyes, hug her as I tried to find the words to express this gift as tears began to fall from my eyes, and tell her how much her voice speaking God's promises over me had saved me. I shared with her that I, too, had suffered through deep depression and was currently beginning to write about my own story. I told her about the attacks of the enemy and his attempts to instill fear within me that, if I told people the truth of what I had been through, I would lose my credibility. Sheila looked straight into my eyes and, with her beautiful Scottish accent declared, "It's exactly the opposite. Your book will free countless people." I received those words as a prophetic truth over this book you now hold. I claim now, as you are reading this, that God is using this book, through His Spirit, to bring you to deeper levels of freedom that He has for you.

This encounter with Sheila Walsh was another step in my healing. This is God's work. I can trust Him. I finally know I'm safe in His arms. It took a long time to get here and I know He's not done with me yet. But this moment was evidence and confirmation to me that He sees me. If you wonder if He sees you in your pain, I hope this helps you to know He does. He will never leave you or forsake you. You can't hide from His love. You can't outrun him, or fool Him, or try to earn your way out of it. Believe me, I've tried. He loves you with an everlasting, reckless love. He'll never give up on you and He'll never stop pursuing you. So don't give up on you either.

Without the experiences of our deepest flaws, we would never know His deepest grace. It's when our gifts and talents aren't enough and our best-laid plans come crashing down, that we know His compassionate love for us best. It's in those moments when the position we find ourselves in seems hopeless and redemption is like a faraway dream, that we cling to His promise, "Never will I leave you. Never will I forsake you." As Sheila pointed out through the life of Peter, it's when the only thing we have left to offer God is the only thing He ever really wanted: our own broken heart. At that moment, we can truly let go of trying to make ourselves and everyone else okay. God's holiness, graciousness, goodness, mercy, and love are a perfect match for our inadequacies.

Our fall; His grace. Our failure; His perfection. Our weakness; His strength. Our lack; His abundance. Our broken hearts; His stable hands.

But he said to me, "My grace is sufficient for you, for my power is made perfect in weakness." Therefore I will boast all the more gladly about my weaknesses, so that Christ's power may rest on me. That is why, for Christ's sake, I delight in weaknesses, in insults, in hardships, in persecutions, in difficulties. For when I am weak, then I am strong.

~ 2 Corinthians 12:9-10

7

Breaking Soul Ties With Myself And Others: Giving And Receiving Forgiveness

I waited patiently for the LORD; He turned to me and heard my cry. He lifted me out of the mud and mire; He set my feet on a rock and gave me a firm place to stand. He put a new song in my mouth, A hymn of praise to our God. Many will see and fear the LORD and put their trust in Him.

~ Psalms 40:1-3

I want to tell you about my process of receiving forgiveness. One area that the enemy used against me for years was my repeated sexual sin. I battled with shame for a very long time due to the accusations of the enemy. But Romans 8:1 says, "Therefore, there is now no condemnation for those who are in Christ Jesus." One morning I was sitting at my kitchen table, and I asked God if He would please forgive me for my past sexual sin, which was an area where I had repeatedly failed Him. I have asked for forgiveness in this area of my life over and over again. That day, I told God I didn't want to go back. I wanted to commit to Him on this day that I desire to and was going to honor Him with my body from this moment on.

As tears streamed down my face, I asked Him if He would please forgive me for all of my past sexual sins once and for all. What I heard in my Spirit immediately shocked me so that I will never forget the moment. I heard God speak to me, "Melissa, those sins are at the bottom of the ocean. I see them no more. When will you forgive yourself?" I immediately realized that God had truly forgiven me. The truth of this struck me so deeply that I began to sob even more. I could tangibly feel the guilt and shame falling off of my body. God had just told me personally what His Word says in Micah 7:19: "You will again have compassion on us; you will tread our sins underfoot and hurl all of our iniquities into the depths of the sea." God had really forgiven me and, this time, I knew it for sure.

Soon after, I found myself one evening lying on the floor of my bedroom crying for the girl I was in college—the girl who didn't yet know who she was and therefore acted out recklessly again and again. My heart began to soften as I started to feel compassion for my former self. I was brought to tears thinking about her and how lost and lonely she was, and I began to pray to God to help me to forgive the girl I used to be. Suddenly, I saw a picture of the girl I was in college in the tight tank top and short skirt. I saw her getting drunk and giving herself away and betraying herself and God. But what struck me most is who I saw right next to her. I saw that Jesus was right there with her. I realized that on that bedroom floor, Jesus had been there the whole time with me, even in the moments I was most ashamed of, He had never left me. He had seen it all and He still loved me.

At this moment, I thought of the Samaritan woman at the well. Jesus had found her at the well at midday and told her all about herself, confirming to her that He is the Messiah that she spoke of. The woman immediately left her water jar, which she had been at the well to fill with physical water, and went back into the town to tell the people about the Living Water she had found: "Come, see a man who told me everything I ever did. Could this be the Messiah?" (John 4:29).

Jesus told me that not only did He forgive me and that He loved me, but He taught me also to forgive my past self because at the time that girl didn't love herself. Jesus can find you in a hospital bed, at the bottom of a bottle, or in a hotel room with a stranger. He can find you standing in front of the mirror naked telling yourself you hate what you see, or running down the street as fast as you can in an attempt to burn those last calories. Jesus can find you when your credit card debt is making you sick, when you're on that application on your phone again searching for love from people who you know will never care about you, or when you're looking at pornography behind closed doors in a dark room.

"For I am convinced that neither death nor life, neither angels nor demons, neither the present nor the future, nor any powers, neither height nor depth, nor anything else in all creation, will be able to separate us from the love of God that is in Christ Jesus our Lord" (Romans 8:38-39).

Despite all of the times I've strayed from God, betrayed Him, and been unfaithful to Him, He has never, not once, strayed from me. No matter how fast I've tried to run away from Him, His pursuit of me was stronger. No matter how desperately I've tried to hide from Him, His desire for me to be found by Him was greater. I've been unable to escape His never-ending love and mercy for me. And that's how He won me. "This is love: not that we loved God, but that he loved us and sent his Son as an atoning sacrifice for our sins" (1 John 4:10).

I failed Him over and over and yet He still loves me. He never left me. This is because the love of God, True Love, keeps no record of wrongs (1 Corinthians 13:5). I realized that, in my continued process of healing, I had many soul ties to break. There were many people, things, behaviors, and patterns that I had unhealthy relationships with, and these had to change.

The prospect of delving deeper into my past for healing was intimidating, but when attaining your freedom becomes more important to you than safeguarding your reputation and your need for your freedom becomes greater than your fear, you will do anything you have to do to get it! God told me, "You will write your way through this. And it won't be just for you. Others' healing journeys will occur through you sharing your testimony." I knew I had to write this book. And Pastor Jamal Miller gave a prophetic word: "That which you wept over has become your praise" and I received it.

One major area I had to break a soul tie with was my own ego and false self-image, as well as my care for the esteem of the world and what the world thinks of me. I replaced these unhealthy soul ties with my identity in Christ.

"For those who are led by the Spirit of God are the children of God. The Spirit you received does not make you slaves, so that you live in fear again; rather, the Spirit you received brought about your adoption to sonship. And by him we cry, 'Abba, Father.' The Spirit Himself testifies with our spirit that we are God's children. Now if we are children, then we are heirs—heirs of God and co-heirs with Christ, if indeed we share in his sufferings in order that we may also share in his glory" (Romans 8:14-17).

God revealed to me that, due to wounds of rejection from my past, I had been living my life through an orphan spirit and sometimes as a slave, rather than as a Child of God. Instead of living from a place of knowing my identity and value as a Daughter of the King, I had often felt that I had to earn the love of God by "being or doing good," or felt like a slave who was in bondage to sins and failures of my past.

During my process of healing, God told me that he was doing *spiritual surgery* on me. God told me, "I'm going to replace the orphan heart with a princess heart." He has done as He said He would, and I now claim fully my position as a Daughter of the King! After having been afraid He would never take me back, He clothed me in a white robe and placed a crown of gold upon my head.

When Peter let down the nets in the morning after Jesus commanded him to do so, it went against everything that his expertise, intellect, skill, and worldly experience taught him. People would surely think he was crazy. What would they say? They would judge him. They would not approve. Against his own personal preferences and ego, Peter did what Jesus said and was blessed with abundance. Everyone connected to Peter was blessed by this abundance. It wasn't really about Peter after all. I might just look like pure craziness to the world. But I don't care anymore. I want God's way. I choose what God already chose for me.

"But God chose the foolish things of the world to shame the wise; God chose the weak things of the world to shame the strong" (1 Corinthians 1:27).

The enemy knows exactly where your trauma wounds are because he had the biggest role in creating them. If you have a wound of rejection, the enemy is going to offer you an anecdote in the form of external validation and approval. He'll use this same tactic over and over, hoping you'll take the bait. Counterfeits smell like external validation and taste like external approval. They appeal to your fleshly senses and make you "look good" in front of other people. They stroke your ego and momentarily fill the void that the rejection wound created.

It's not enough to get rid of the counterfeits (the bait of the enemy). We need to break off and cast and command out the root of rejection and all of its familiar spirits. In breaking soul ties, we also need to forgive those who have harmed us and disappointed us. We need to release bitterness and the need for approval and validation from external sources. We need to release pride and embrace humility. We are doing this so we can discontinue past unhealthy patterns for good. We won't be deceived again. When you know you are forgiven, redeemed, and restored, the enemy can no longer hold your testimony hostage!

It took me and the Lord six months of deep deliverance work to heal from my past. The Lord freed me from generational curses (alcoholism, food addiction, insecure attachment, divorce, scarcity); spirit of isolation (depression, and anxiety); orphan spirit (spirit of self-reliance, pride); false self-image (ego, fear of man); co-dependency (spirit of false responsibility, spirit of control, breaking unhealthy soul ties with family members, friends, ex-boyfriends, and anyone with whom I've had sexual relationships). I broke off the lie that I had to earn love and that God was going to reject and/or abandon me.

Jesus is the same yesterday, today, and forever. He is the same God Who brought me from a lower-class family to earn three university degrees. He is the same God Who delivered me from the depths of depression and the pit of death. He is the same God Who built my successful business when I came from no business background or experience. He is the same God Who brought me into The One University, a ministry to prepare for Godly marriage, when I pleaded on my knees that I had no idea how to have healthy relationships with men and surrendered. He is the same God Who delivered me from strongholds that have been generational and lifelong. He is the same God Who rescued me from insecure attachment, co-dependency, addictions, self-hatred, perfectionism, guilt, shame, and fear. He is the same God Who saved my father's life last year. He is the same God Who forgave me everything and gave me a new name. He is the same God Who restored my identity. He is the same God Who has turned and is turning the places in my life where I saw ashes into beauty. He is the same God Who is giving me the courage to share my story with others. He is the same God Who is teaching me to open my heart to receive healthy love from my future husband. He is the same God Who is giving me hope that someday I will have a family of my own.

An important moment in my healing from my past and in my asking for and receiving forgiveness was with my father. I had continued to carry guilt and shame that I had not listened to the wisdom and instruction of my father when he tried to tell me to slow down and that I didn't have to get married so quickly. For years afterward, I felt a deep sense of disappointment and regret within myself that I had not listened to my father and, in doing so, I had not only harmed myself greatly, but I had brought pain upon my entire family.

While walking outside one day, I called my father. I started the conversation by telling him I needed to ask him something. Then I proceeded to talk to him about my regrets from the past and how I wish I had taken his advice. He cut in and said to me, "What is it you want to ask me?" I began to cry. I asked him, "Dad, will you please forgive me for not listening to you?" He immediately said, "That's what I thought you were going to ask. Of course, I forgive you. We have all made mistakes. Now it's time for you to let it go, and to move forward." As soon as I heard these words from my earthly father, I felt a shift in my spirit. After I said "I love you" and hanging up the phone, the Holy Spirit revealed to me this shift. I had just seen, manifested in the physical realm with my earthly father, a picture of my relationship with my Heavenly Father. Just as my earthly father in his grace, compassion, mercy, and kindness, had forgiven me immediately, as soon as I asked, so has my Heavenly Father. This short conversation released me from years of internal bondage.

After I finally accepted forgiveness from the Lord, I wanted to get baptized. This was my testimony for my baptism:

I've gone to church from a very young age. I was christened as a baby and was saved and baptized in middle school, but it was only just recently that I gave all the broken parts of my whole heart to Jesus.

In my twenties, when I was in graduate school, I fell off a third story building because of alcohol intoxication and a broken fire escape, but God saved my life. I remember waking up in a hospital bed the next morning not being able to move and being afraid that I might never walk again or think the same way again. But I was alive. And I knew I was going to be okay. I later found out that my brain was not bleeding, I hadn't broken a single bone in my body. The Lord told me then, "This is how much I love you." I know angels caught me that night.

In my thirties, after I earned my doctorate, I ran ahead of God, married the wrong person, and endured an abusive relationship which led me into severe clinical depression and hospitalization. I was completely humiliated and hopeless. In my darkest moments of suffering and in the depths of severe depression, PTSD, and isolation, Jesus has always been there with me. When I have been unfaithful to Him and betrayed Him and myself over and over, He has never left me because His Name is Faithful and True.

The enemy lied to me and told me that I was disqualified and I had forfeited the purpose, calling, and plan that God has for my life because of how much I've failed. But God told me: "My grace is sufficient for you, for my power is made perfect in weakness." And "The gifts and callings of the Lord are irrevocable."

The enemy told me I had made too many mistakes and God didn't love me anymore and I was going to be alone forever, but God told me "I will never leave you or forsake you," and Jesus told me, "To her who has been forgiven much; loves much."

The enemy told me that I should give up because I'm never going to be healed and I'm always going to be broken. But Jesus said to me, "Who the Son sets free, is free indeed!" And "By his stripes I AM HEALED!" And "I can do all things through Christ who strengthens me!" And "In Jesus Christ I am MORE than a conqueror!"

I'm getting baptized today because I have decided to give Jesus Christ my entire heart and my entire life and I'm declaring today that I am forever His and He is forever mine. And I will not die but LIVE and I WILL proclaim what the LORD has done! I am redeemed, restored, and renewed today because of the price that Jesus paid!

My name is Melissa, and today I declare that JESUS IS LORD. This day of baptism as an adult and making the public decision to re-commit my life to Jesus was the best day of my life.

You see, I thought I had lost the opportunity to have the life God wanted me to have. I thought I'd missed it entirely. I thought my mistakes were too many, and my fall from grace was too far. But God knew the mistakes I was going to make before I made them, and He already had a plan to get me back on track before I ever got off track.

The enemy will try to condemn you with lies that you are too lost and too far off track in your life to ever get back to the purposes that God predestined for your life. But I'm writing this book to tell you that is a lie from the pit of hell. God's gifts and his call are irrevocable. (Romans 11:29). The moment you turn back to Him is the very moment God runs toward you!

This is depicted by Jesus in The Parable of the Prodigal Son.

And when he came to himself, he said, How many hired servants of my father's have bread enough and to spare, and I perish with hunger!

[18] I will arise and go to my father, and will say unto him, Father, I have sinned against heaven, and before thee,

[19] And am no more worthy to be called thy son: make me as one of thy hired servants.

²⁰ And he arose, and came to his father. But when he was yet a great way off, his father saw him, and had compassion, and ran, and fell on his neck, and kissed him.

²¹ And the son said unto him, Father, I have sinned against heaven, and in thy sight, and am no more worthy to be called thy son.

²² But the father said to his servants, Bring forth the best robe, and put it on him; and put a ring on his hand, and shoes on his feet:

²³ And bring hither the fatted calf, and kill it; and let us eat, and be merry:

²⁴ For this my son was dead, and is alive again; he was lost, and is found. And they began to be merry.

~ Luke 15:17-24

It's in your moments of greatest humiliation—when you have squandered the resources you've been given, embarrassed yourself, and disgraced your family. It's the moment when you are so disappointed in yourself that you are afraid to let your best friends know the mistakes that you've made. It's when you realize that you used to be the one that people would look to for help and guidance and now you are suddenly the one who is powerless and hopeless. It's when the entire profession and career that you have built up your whole life is crumbling around you. It's when your marriage breaks up, your home is foreclosed on, and bankruptcy is looming. It's when you feel certain that you'll never be in an esteemed position again and you think you've used up your very last chance. This is when your enemy wants you to believe that God no longer loves you, that He is angry with you and ashamed of you. But this is also the moment when the mercy and grace of God come pouring forth. This is the way it was for me.

Your enemy doesn't want you to know that God rescued you, and he certainly doesn't want you to believe that, because God saved you, He is also going to secure you and direct you. The truth is that God has saved and secured you and now He is bringing to pass his plans and purposes for your life. "He lifted me out of the mud and mire; He set my feet on a rock and gave me a firm place to stand" (Psalms 40:2).

This is not in spite of what you've been through, but God is going to integrate every moment of suffering into your testimony and make you stronger and more powerful in Him than ever before, if you will only have faith in Him to do so. If you'll just trust Him at His Word, and who He says He is, I Am That I AM. The Great I AM will take everything the enemy has stolen from you and use it for his purpose and for your good. There is nothing our God can't do.

If you have found yourself lost and off course and nothing in your life has turned out the way you thought it would, the only thing that you have to do is turn around and run directly back into his arms. He will put a new song in your mouth. (Psalms 40:3). He will replace your ashes with a crown of beauty. (Isaiah 61:3)

God is calling your name out loud right now. Can you hear Him? He is telling you He still has a plan and a purpose for your life and none of the suffering that you've been through will be in vain. He is calling you by name back to Himself. You know you were meant for so much more. God still wants to use you. It's not too late. How will you respond?

[29] For whom he did foreknow, he also did predestinate to be conformed to the image of his Son, that he might be the firstborn among many brethren.

[30] Moreover whom he did predestinate, them he also called: and whom he called, them he also justified: and whom he justified, them he also glorified.

~ Romans 8:29-30

It wasn't until I finally realized that God didn't call me in spite of my failures and imperfections, God called me *because of* my failures and imperfections. He justified me before I ever made the mistakes He knew I was going to make. When I realized that this was the kind of God that I serve Who would take all of my failures, embarrassments, humiliation, and mistakes, and find another way to get me to my purpose, and would never give up on me, God changed my entire understanding of who He is.

I had always believed that I had to earn it, but God has made it clear to me that the purposes He has for my life would never be something that I could attain with my own strength, power, or goodness; God's purposes are only manifested through His strength, His power, and His goodness.

8

Goodbye Addictions, Obsessions, And Compulsions

So if the son sets you free, you will be free indeed.

~ John 8:36

Have you ever been in a situation where you were overly dependent on something as a means of getting through life? Perhaps it was a chemical addiction—alcohol, drugs, or food. Or
perhaps it was a behavioral addiction—spending, gambling,
pornography, masturbation, or sex. Perhaps your addiction
has been in relationships—co-dependency. Or perhaps your
addiction comes in the form of a subtler pattern of behavior
that is socially acceptable such as performance and achievement addiction (workaholic); validation and approval addic-

tion (people-pleasing), or perfectionism—needing to have the perfect home, career, relationship, children, appearance, and Instagram posts.

Addiction (as defined by the DSM-5) is:

A maladaptive pattern of substance abuse leading to clinically significant impairment or distress, as manifested by 2 (or more) of the following, occurring within a 12-month period: Recurrent use resulting in failure to fulfill major role obligations; recurrent use in hazardous situations; continued use despite negative consequences; increased tolerance of the substance; withdrawal from the substance; substance taken longer than intended; unsuccessful attempts to control use; much time spent to obtain and/or recover from, substance; other activities and relationships are given up; use continues in spite of recurrent physical and/or psychological problems; cravings, strong desire to use the substance (obsession).

Addiction can be both physiological and/or psychological dependence on a behavior or substance. Behavioral addictions can include such things as sex, pornography, gambling, spending, relationships—co-dependency, obsessive internet use—social media. Addictions can be consumptive or "chemical" addictions (alcohol, drugs, food—anorexia, bulimia, binge eating, compulsive overeating).

Consider that addiction is akin to spiritual suicide. Addiction in a spiritual sense is anything or anyone that we place above God. Anything or anyone that we make an idol of and place on the throne of our hearts instead of God Himself might be categorized as an addiction. This sin does not allow the level of intimacy with God that He desires to enjoy with us. it could be anything from a relationship with someone to a need for constant validation on social media and self-exultation. Just consider our current world of "selfies." In a spiritual sense then, the opposite of addiction (which is an unhealthy disconnection from God, one's own spirit, and others), is a healthy connection and relationship with God, ourselves, and others.

Whatever it is you struggle with—and whether you see it as a dependency, which you feel you still have some control over, or an addiction, where you experience a complete lack of control and choice, I know what it feels like to grapple with the realization that you have a problem. I know what it's like to be afraid to admit the problem, most of all to yourself. I also know the process of denial and bargaining, because when you actually admit to yourself that you really have a problem, you are then faced with the reality that you might need to make a change. This problem, although it has caused negative consequences in your life, is also something that you have come to depend on, and the struggle to let it go is real.

Many of the chemical and behavioral addictions we face as human beings are due to subconscious beliefs we hold about ourselves. By subconscious beliefs, I am referring to beliefs that we hold about ourselves that we are not consciously aware of. Consider the notion of an iceberg in the ocean. Most of the iceberg is actually submerged underneath the water. We are able to see and be aware of only that part of the iceberg that is above the surface. However, there is a large amount of ice beneath the water that we would not be aware of without further exploration. Our thought life is similar. We have our conscious thoughts, which we are aware of day to day, moment to moment. These thoughts are the part of the iceberg that we can "see" above the surface of the water. We can notice our thoughts at the moment, and we have the ability to "think about our thinking." This is called metacognition. But it is our subconscious beliefs, those beliefs we have "below the surface," that actually drive our conscious thoughts.

Now that we understand that our unconscious thoughts and beliefs drive our conscious thoughts, we need to also understand that our conscious thoughts are responsible for our emotional life. Our mind, that is our thoughts, impact how we feel. Moreover, our emotions (how we feel) are often what drive our behaviors. Finally, our behaviors are what produce results and consequences in our lives. If we follow this thread through, we see that it is our subconscious beliefs that are actually at the root of what we manifest in our lives. This is aligned with the scripture: For as he thinks in his heart, so *is* he. "Eat and drink!" he says to you, But his heart is not with you. (Proverbs 23:7).

The Bible says: "Do not conform to the pattern of this world, but be transformed by the renewing of your mind. Then you will be able to test and approve what God's will is—his good, pleasing and perfect will" (Romans 12:2). If you want your *life* to be transformed from the inside out, and you desire a true inner transformation that will bring you sustainable fruit and the manifestation of blessings that God has in store for you, then you must make a habit of continuously renewing your mind with truth. This is not a one-and-done type of renewal. This is a moment-by-moment renewal. This is a lifelong pursuit.

We must become experts in taking inventory of, assessing, and monitoring our own conscious thoughts and we must be willing to go through a deep process of deliverance to allow God to uproot and restructure our subconscious beliefs that are not in alignment with His truth. As many of our subconscious beliefs are rooted in past trauma and woundedness, it is essential that we undertake this process because otherwise our lives are built on a foundation of lies.

Experts estimate that the mind thinks between 60,000 and 80,000 thoughts per day. That's an average of 2,500 to 3,300 thoughts per hour. That would be 41 thoughts per minute, or about 7/10 of a thought every second. Do you recognize how powerful your mind is? If we are to truly do what the Bible is telling us to do, that would be to *continually* assess our thoughts. 2 Corinthians 10:5 tells us: "We demolish arguments and every pretension that sets itself up against the knowledge of God, and we take captive *every thought* to make it obedient to Christ." Notice that this scripture does not say every emotion, or every behavior, or even every result, consequence, or outcome. The scripture says we take captive every *thought*. This is because God knows the power of our thoughts.

God knows that our thoughts create our lives. "Death and life is in the power of the tongue" (Proverbs 18:20). "A good man out of the good treasure of his heart brings forth good; and an evil man out of the evil treasure of his heart brings forth evil. For out of the abundance of the heart his mouth speaks" (Luke 6:45). The heart, (our thought life), is also responsible for what we speak, and God spoke the world into being. "For He spoke, and it was *done;* He commanded, and it stood fast" (Psalms 33:9).

God knows our thoughts before we think them, knows our behaviors before we do them, and knows our words before we speak them.

> *"Lord, you have examined me*
> *and know all about me.*
> *You know when I sit down and when I get up.*
> *You know my thoughts before I think them.*
> *You know where I go and where I lie down.*
> *You know everything I do.*
> *Lord, even before I say a word,*
> *you already know it."*

~ Psalms 139:1-4

God knows our hearts better than we do. "Now He who searches the hearts knows what the mind of the Spirit is, because He makes intercession for the saints according to the will of God" (Romans 8:28). Jesus, our eternal high priest, lives to make intercession for us. "Now there have been many of those priests, since death prevented them from continuing in office; but because Jesus lives forever, he has a permanent priesthood. Therefore, he is able to save completely those who come to God through him, because he always lives to intercede for them" (Hebrews 7:23-25).

Although the enemy can try to attack our minds by whispering lies into our ears, the enemy does not, as God does, know our thoughts before we think them. Therefore, one of our greatest weapons against the enemy is our thought life! We can trick the enemy by changing the patterns of our thoughts! By dwelling on God's truths instead of the lies of the enemy, by healing our trauma, by uprooting the negative self-beliefs that have been formed due to the trauma of our pasts, and being delivered from the lies we've believed about God, our lives, and other people, we have the power to overcome the enemy by truly being transformed by the renewing of our minds. We have so much power through God's Holy Spirit to wage war against the enemy by becoming masters over our minds through replacing lies we tell ourselves with God's truth!

John 1:1-5 tells us: "In the beginning was the Word, and the Word was with God, and the Word was God. He was with

God in the beginning. Through him all things were made; without him, nothing was made that has been made. In him was life, and that life was the light of all mankind. The light shines in the darkness, and the darkness has not overcome it." John goes on to say in Chapter 1:14: "The Word became flesh and made his dwelling among us. We have seen his glory, the glory of the one and only Son, who came from the Father, full of grace and truth."

"Jesus, the Word, was with God from the beginning, and was God from the beginning. Nothing has been created without him, and nothing exists apart from him. The darkness within you cannot overcome the light that God has placed within you through his son, Jesus. Rather, God's Holy Spirit within you will one day overcome all darkness within you, and God will complete His good work that he has begun in you" (Philippians 1:6).

"Therefore, if anyone is in Christ, the new creation has come. The old has gone, the new is here! All this is from God, who reconciled us to Himself through Christ and gave us the ministry of reconciliation: that God was reconciling the world to Himself in Christ, not counting people's sins against them. And he has committed to us the message of reconciliation. We are therefore Christ's ambassadors, as though God were making his appeal through us. We implore you on Christ's behalf: Be reconciled to God. God made him who had no sin to become sin for us, so that in him we might become the righteousness of God" (2 Corinthians 5:17-21).

Every proclivity, obsession, compulsion, crutch, dependency, and addiction that you struggle with must bow down to be overcome by the Blood of Jesus. As you take your victory through Christ, God will use every moment that you spent in those ungodly activities and harness that energy back to saving and helping others through you. After God rescues you, he will use you to rescue others. You can't save others until you know what it is to be saved. Nothing you have battled through on your journey to freedom will be wasted. God will use it all!

Jesus told us in John 16:33: "I have told you these things, so that in me you may have peace. In this world you will have trouble. But take heart! I have overcome the world!" It is completed. It is finished. It has already happened in the spirit realm. Jesus has already overcome the world and with it He will also overcome every struggle within you that you face in your flesh while you are still in the world but not of the world. And therefore, Jesus commands us to "take heart."

In her beautiful classic book, *The God of All Comfort*, Hannah Whitall Smith writes: "… 'Be of good cheer' is the command of the Lord for His disciples, always and under all circumstances; and He founded this command on the tremendous fact that He has overcome the world, and that therefore there was nothing left for us to be discouraged about. As I have said before, if we only understood what it means that Christ has overcome the world, I believe we would be aghast at the very idea of any one of His followers ever being discouraged again" (pp. 187-188).

Although we are in the world, we are told, "Do not love the world or anything in the world. If anyone loves the world, love for the Father is not in them. For everything in the world—the lust of the flesh, the lust of the eyes, and the pride of life—comes not from the Father but from the world. The world and its desires pass away, but whoever does the will of God lives forever" (1 John 2: 15-17). Consider how the enemy uses the lust of the flesh, the lust of the eyes, and the pride of life to tempt us into cycles of addiction and bondage, often in generational cycles.

When I started praying consistently for self-control, my entire life changed. "For God gave us a spirit not of fear but of power, and love, and self-control" (2 Timothy 1:7). With the Holy Spirit living within us, we are able to possess self-control, and demonstrate the fruits of the Spirit of self-control. As a result of this self-control through the power of God's Spirit, we can defeat all addictions and live in the abundant life and freedom that Jesus has paid the price for us to receive! Jesus says: "The thief does not come except to steal, and to kill, and to destroy. I have come that they may have life, and that they may have *it* more abundantly" (John 10:10). An abundant life is a life of spiritual freedom!

Do not underestimate the power of God's Holy Spirit in you to drastically change your lifelong thought and behavioral patterns. "Ask, and it will be given to you; seek, and you will find; knock, and it will be opened to you" (Matthew 7:7). As a result of our asking, God will transform our lives into lives that are pleasing and honorable to Him! This includes self-control over, and freedom from, addictions to food, alcohol, drugs, overspending, need to control outcomes and circumstances (which often leads to anxiety, doubt, fear, and depression), approval and validation addiction, co-dependency (needing to control others), relationship addiction, perfectionism, workaholism, self and body hatred, eating disorders (binging and restricting), exercise addiction, sexual addictions, pornography and masturbation, gambling, and anything else that might be taking the place of God on the throne of our hearts, and being an idol in our lives.

I am going to share how God delivered me from multiple areas of bondage in my life in order to be a witness to the power of God's Holy Spirit working within my own life and as a means of providing you with practical strategies that may help you in walking out your own freedom journey that God has already prepared for you. I share this with you in prayer that it will be of benefit to you and God will use it to help to set you free from areas of bondage that you may have been struggling with for years, as I did. Therefore, I will tell you plainly the ways God worked in my life to free me.

"And so it was with me, brothers and sisters. When I came to you, I did not come with eloquence or human wisdom as I proclaimed to you the testimony about God. For I resolved to know nothing while I was with you except Jesus Christ and him crucified. I came to you in weakness with great fear and trembling. My message and my preaching were not with wise and persuasive words, but with a demonstration of the Spirit's power, so that your faith might not be in human wisdom, but on God's power" (1 Corinthians 2:1-5).

The *only* reason I am where I am, in my life at this moment, is because of the Power of God working in and through me. As I began my journey to freedom in multiple areas of my life, Jesus told me that He was giving me *His* actual freedom. When I heard this in my spirit, I asked Him how this could be possible with all of my shortcomings, mistakes, and lack of faith. Jesus told me that my freedom is not dependent upon me, but it is dependent upon Him. It is His freedom that I now experience. It is the very same experience of freedom that Jesus Himself experiences. This is the expression of His Spirit. "Now the Lord is the Spirit, and where the Spirit of the Lord is, there is freedom" (2 Corinthians 3:17). It is important to underscore that I could have never earned or worked to achieve the freedom that I now enjoy in my life. It's the freedom of Christ, given to me by His Spirit that I am sharing with you. It's His very experience of freedom that I now enjoy.

MONEY

After my divorce, and moving into my own apartment, I found myself in a situation a year later in which I had a great amount of credit card debt. I discovered that I did not make enough of a salary teaching at the university to support myself and my bills and each month I found myself getting further and further into debt. On top of growing credit card bills, I also had a car loan and student loans from my undergraduate studies I was still paying off. I felt myself drowning in debt and I saw no way out. I knew that I wasn't making enough money to support my lifestyle and I was not managing my money the best I could. I had no structure in terms of a budget or a plan to get out of debt. I felt overwhelmed at the prospect of trying to get hold of my finances and did not know where to begin. I realized that I was now $24,000 in credit card debt. I was embarrassed and humiliated by my irresponsibility and lack of knowledge about how to help myself out of this bondage.

It was at that time that I began to cry out to God for help with my finances. I had no idea in what form God would send me this help but I knew I could not manage this on my own. It was perhaps a week or two later, after praying for help in the area of my finances, that I was sitting in church at the beginning of the service and there was an announcement for an upcoming class that would be offered at the church called "Financial Peace University" by Dave Ramsey. I knew at that very moment that this was God answering my prayer. I signed up for the class immediately and began my journey with others in my church toward financial freedom.

During the eight weeks of class, I learned invaluable lessons about how God sees money. I learned the importance of

being a good steward of the finances that God has entrust-
ed to me. I learned how to create a budget and stick to it. I
learned the power of the "debt snowball." I received support
and encouragement from other people who were in all kinds
of different financial situations and there was no judgment or
condemnation, only help and support.

I continued to work full time at the university while
building my private clinical mental health counseling practice on the side. In the beginning, I worked on Fridays in my
private practice. Soon, I had so many clients that my Fridays
were full, and so I began to work on Saturdays. as well. Soon,
my Saturdays were also full. I continued to work two jobs
and my discipline in my financial life took on a new level that
I had never before experienced. A year and a half later, I was
completely out of credit card debt and my car was completely
paid off. Now I am working on paying off my school loans
and then I will be entirely debt-free!

Along with going through Financial Peace University
(FPU) at my church, I also saw a post on social media by a
friend of mine who was interested in helping people (free of
charge) by providing them financial counseling and mentor-
ship. This friend has worked with me to set up budgets and
financial goals for my personal life and business and has continued to support me and check in with me over the past two
years. In addition, a friend I met through FPU has become
my business bookkeeper and has been a major source of support in helping me to manage my successful counseling prac-

tice. All of these blessings came into my life from God simply because I asked for His help. I am so incredibly grateful for all of the ways that God has brought financial freedom into my life. I want to encourage you because this is possible for you as well!

FOOD AND ALCOHOL

As discussed previously in this book, food and alcohol are things that I have struggled with at various times throughout my life. Up until the past couple of years, I am not sure that I have ever had a healthy relationship with food. Growing up as an overweight child was at the root of many of my issues with rejection. Even when I had lost weight, I still struggled to embrace and celebrate my body. Even at my thinnest and most toned, I still found fault with my body. I have vacillated between seasons of restriction through diets and intense amounts of exercise and seasons of giving in to complete lack of control by overindulging in food and falling away from exercise. I have lost weight and gained it back over and over again. It was not until I made the connection between food and my emotional, psychological, and spiritual self and prayed to ask God for support that I finally became free.

Two winters ago, as I started to fall into a depression, I realized that I needed to get back to structured workouts, not so much for my physical health, but for the benefits to my mental health. When my sister introduced me to a local gym called The Body Architect (BA) and gifted me with a free one-month membership, I weighed about 20 pounds more than I currently weigh. At The BA, I was met with one-on-one and had semi-private weight training sessions with trainers who encouraged me to increase strength, endurance, and flexibility, all in a safe atmosphere of non-judgment. There is not one scale in the entire building. For once in my life, my exercise routine did not focus on the weight on the scale, but on an overall level of health. I looked forward to my scheduled workouts each week and began to feel my mental health and physical strength improve. I felt a sense of community with the trainers and the other participants, and this sense of community kept me engaged and accountable. I met with a personal trainer once per week for an accountability coaching session to discuss my progress.

The next blessing in this area of my life that God provided was personal health coaching. One of my friends from church who happens to be a massage therapist called me one day out of the blue. My friend told me that she had a friend she worked with who was completing her internship to become a certified health coach and needed a client to work with free of charge, and she went on to tell me that I immediately came to mind. There was a moment on the phone when I hesitated about receiving this help, and then God brought back to my remembrance my prayer for support. I said yes. Over the next five months, I met weekly with my very own health coach, completely free of charge. My health coach not only worked with me on physical health and nutrition, but also supported my emotional, psychological, and spiritual goals and wellbeing. I know beyond a shadow of a doubt that this free gift of health coaching was a blessing in my life from God to continue to help free me from many lifelong patterns and struggles when it came to food, alcohol, body image, self-love, and relationships. I will be forever grateful for the time I was so fortunate to work with Tammy.

Since this time, I have stopped drinking alcohol, except for socially and on special occasions, I have stopped eating sugar and processed carbohydrates, I have developed a deeper connection to and love for my body and for what it truly needs to soothe itself and repair itself such as daily exercise, organic whole foods, rest, healthy connection with God and other people, and good sleep. Instead of reaching for unhealthy food or alcohol to soothe and nurture myself, I now reach for what is healthy. I have lost 20 pounds and have kept it off. This is not a fad diet, but rather, a forever lifestyle change. I now know what is healthy for me and I continue to make the best choices daily that align with what is healthiest for myself and my body. This is a form of self-love. My self-worth has flourished from the inside out.

SEX AND MASTURBATION

I lived in the realm of my flesh in the area of sexual promiscuity and masturbation for many years. Just as Romans 8:5-8 tells us: "Those who live according to the flesh have their minds set on what the flesh desires; but those who live in accordance with the Spirit have their minds set on what the

Spirit desires. The mind governed by the flesh is death, but the mind governed by the Spirit is life and peace. The mind governed by the flesh is hostile to God; it does not submit to God's law, nor can it do so. Those who are in the realm of the flesh cannot please God."

I earnestly believed that the only way that I would be able to receive love from a man was by giving myself to him physically. I was living under deception in this area of my life and I honestly did not believe I was worthy of anything more. I was afraid of true emotional vulnerability, of truly being seen, and therefore I hid behind a facade of intimacy through sexuality.

I have held the most shame and guilt in this area of my life, and it is of no surprise to me that this section of this book has been the section that I am most afraid to write about. I have spent a lifetime fearing judgment because of my sexual sin, both from God and from other people.

But when I prayed about writing this section of the book, God told me to write about resurrection. He told me to tell you how He resurrected me from the pit of death and brought me to a place of new life in him. I never realized that I would actually be able to get all of the parts of myself back that I had given away through having sex with so many different people.

I did not know that I could actually be made pure once again. This was a stumbling block and a place of condemnation that the enemy has held against me for years. It was even so much of a hindrance to me that the enemy has used it against me to make me call into question my salvation. I have been in a place of torment and despair, at times doubting whether I would even be saved because of my sexual sin.

Once I realized that my sexual recklessness and acting out was not soothing me, satisfying me, or providing me with anything that I needed, but rather was actually a form of self-harm, is when I stopped. When I realized that the severe emotional and psychological pain that I was causing myself was worse than the fear that God would not forgive me and restore this area of my life, I cried out for help. I asked the Lord to please help me to discontinue this pattern of self-inflicted abuse in my life. And He answered me.

I later learned that I could not only pray a prayer that would completely break off soul ties with past sexual partners, but I could also repent and ask God to return all of the parts of myself due to the soul ties I had formed, and make me whole again. This process of breaking soul ties and asking God to bring back parts of myself that I thought I had lost forever took months. But I trusted that He could do it and believed He would do it. One day, while I was praying, I felt a shift not only in my spirit, but in my entire being. I felt the Holy Spirit say to me: "It is as you have asked." And at that moment I knew what He meant: All of the parts of myself that I had lost had now been returned to me.

I could hardly believe it, this feeling that came over me. Something I never thought would be possible for someone like me, with so many mistakes in the beds of so many men who never actually loved me. But what was accomplished through one man who died and rose again, not only freed me but brought me back to a place of purity and wholeness before Him. There is no other explanation I have other than to tell you that Jesus freed me, and Jesus made me whole.

Jesus is the reason I am no longer in the bondage of sexual sin and He is also the reason I have the confidence to tell you my story in this area because I no longer carry shame and guilt. I know that Jesus did this for me because He loves me, and there is no fear in love. Perfect love casts out fear. (1 John 4:18).

If you are struggling or have struggled with sexual sin in the past and acting out sexually and recklessly has become a form of self-harm to you, I want to encourage you. God has not forgotten you and He will not leave you in the pit that you are in. Ask Him for His help to free you. He is faithful. You are reading this now for a reason. I have struggled in this area of my life, for most of my life, and now I can say that I am free! I have been abstinent from sex for almost three years now.

For many years before this, I was just as Paul stated: "I do not understand what I do. For what I want to do I do not do, but what I hate I do. And if I do what I do not want to do,

I agree that the law is good. As it is, it is no longer I myself who do it, but it is sin living in me. For I know that good itself does not dwell in me, that is, in my sinful nature. For I have the desire to do what is good, but I cannot carry it out. For I do not do the good I want to do, but the evil I do not want to do—this I keep on doing. Now if I do what I do not want to do, it is no longer I who do it, but it is sin living in me that does it" (Romans 7:15-20).

In my own flesh, I was unable to defeat sexual temptation and sin. But that which I was powerless over on my own, with God's Spirit living within me, I had the victory, because with God all things are possible. (Matthew 19:26). When I recognized that I no longer had to be bound by the realm of my flesh, but could take hold of the power in the realm of the Spirit, over the sin of my flesh, I began to experience freedom. "You, however, are not in the realm of the flesh but are in the realm of the Spirit, if indeed the Spirit of God lives in you. And if anyone does not have the Spirit of Christ, they do not belong to Christ" (Romans 8:9).

I began to see the message of the gospel come alive in my life when I recognized that Jesus has already overcome the world (John 16:33), and that truth is present for me in my life today. There is no sin that I can be tempted with, that I am not already victorious over through Christ Jesus living in me. With this truth, I began to proclaim victory in faith over things that were still tempting me and, as I did this, the temptation fled. "Submit yourselves, then, to God. Resist the devil, and he will flee from you" (James 4:7).

The plain truth of the matter is: "If God is for us, who can be against us?" (Romans 8:31). "No weapon formed against you shall prosper" (Isaiah 54:17). You are victorious over sexual sin now in Christ Jesus, because "you are more than a conqueror through him who loves you" (Romans 8:37).

Please remember then, dear reader, that this battle is not yours, but God's. And, because this is a spiritual battle, we are victorious "… 'Not by might nor by power, but by my Spirit', says the LORD Almighty" (Zechariah 4:6). So put on the full armor of God to fight this battle: "Finally, be strong in the Lord and in his mighty power. Put on the full armor of God, so that you can take your stand against the devil's schemes. For our struggle is not against flesh and blood, but against the rulers, against the authorities, against the powers of this dark world and against the spiritual forces of evil in the heavenly realms. Therefore put on the full armor of God, so that when the day of evil comes, you may be able to stand your ground, and after you have done everything, to stand. Stand firm then, with the belt of truth buckled around your waist, with the breastplate of righteousness in place, and with your feet fitted with the readiness that comes from the gospel of peace. In addition to all this, take up the shield of faith, with which you can extinguish all the flaming arrows of the evil one. Take the helmet of salvation and the sword of the Spirit, which is the word of God. And pray in the Spirit on all occasions with all kinds of prayers and requests. With this in mind, be alert and always keep on praying for all the Lord's people" (Ephesians 6:10-18).

Psalms 143
A psalm of David.

Lord, hear my prayer,
listen to my cry for mercy;
in your faithfulness and righteousness
come to my relief.
Do not bring your servant into judgment,
for no one living is righteous before you.
The enemy pursues me,
he crushes me to the ground;
he makes me dwell in the darkness
like those long dead.
So my spirit grows faint within me;
my heart within me is dismayed.
I remember the days of long ago;
I meditate on all your works
and consider what your hands have done.
I spread out my hands to you;
I thirst for you like a parched land.

Answer me quickly, Lord;
my spirit fails.
Do not hide your face from me

or I will be like those who go down to the pit.
Let the morning bring me word of your unfailing love,
for I have put my trust in you.
Show me the way I should go,
for to you I entrust my life.
Rescue me from my enemies, Lord,
for I hide myself in you.
Teach me to do your will,
for you are my God;
may your good Spirit
lead me on level ground.

For your name's sake, Lord, preserve my life;
in your righteousness, bring me out of trouble.

In your unfailing love, silence my enemies;
destroy all my foes,
for I am your servant.

RELATIONSHIP ADDICTION/CO-DEPENDENCY

Relationship addiction or co-dependency is rooted in the lie that someone else can provide the safety, love, and security to us that only God Himself can provide. The lie is often rooted in wounds of early rejection and abandonment by both self and others. There is a deep belief that God would not actually provide us with his complete safety, love, and security because we are undeserving and unworthy and, therefore, we must search endlessly for this from other people.

I always knew there was something broken or missing inside of me, but I could never really put my finger on what it was. I knew that I secretly feared that people would leave me. The terror of this in romantic relationships became so frightening to me that I would go to great lengths to attempt to stop it from happening. If there is any one secret shame that I have so deeply hidden, if there is one deception so sly, that even I did not know where it came from, it is the addiction of co-dependency.

Co-dependency puts one in the position to accept less than what one deserves in a relationship because of fear of losing what one has. The mindset is, "I'd rather try harder even though this is unhealthy than lose what I've already invested in this relationship." It is also the belief, "I'm only okay if those I love are okay." And, "It's my job to make sure others are okay."

Those of us with a history of co-dependency have learned to be experts in holding other people's emotions and attempting to fix situations around us. Unfortunately, to be experts in meeting other people's needs and preferences, people with co-dependent patterns must reject and forfeit our needs and preferences. Many who struggle with co-dependent patterns in relationships may not even know what their own needs and preferences truly are. This is because, to be the expert in meeting everyone else's needs, it is impossible to have and meet your own needs.

Breaking free of co-dependency in relationships is by far the deepest and most difficult addiction that I have had to heal from because it was integral to my very being. It is the way that I had operated in relationships. It was my pattern in romantic relationships and even in some platonic friendships as well. I have had to delve into the deepest layers of where and how co-dependent patterns were formed in my life. The only way out was through. I have had to surrender to God in order to be delivered from these patterns and to walk out, albeit at times clumsily, into new ways of being with God, with myself, and with others.

This journey has been the most frightening and most empowering one of my life. It has left me in places of utter dependency on God and has revamped and realigned my entire mind, body, and soul. One of the greatest lessons I have learned on my journey of recovery is that we are accountable to others, but we are not responsible for others. Reading the book Boundaries by Dr. Cloud and Dr. Townsend took me months and changed my entire life. Each one of us has free will to make our own choices and we all must also face the consequences of those choices. It is not my job to rescue others from the consequences of their own choices, and it is no one else's job to rescue me. We do reap what we sow. (Galatians 6:7).

The truth is that most of what you're worried about isn't even your responsibility. None of what you're worried about is what God commanded you should do. All of what you're worried about is in God's hands.

I recently cried out to God in complete emotional exhaustion saying, "Lord I can't fix them. I can't do it. And I'm sick of trying." God's response in my spirit was quick: "I never asked you to fix them. I asked you to love them. Fixing them is about you. Loving them is about me."

Then I had to pray, "Lord, I die to that part of myself that wants to fix them. I kill that part of myself and I surrender to you. Lord, give me the grace to simply love them." I used to think that I had to try to "fix" people to help them. But now I know that I just have to love them. Jesus can work better in the people that we want to minister to when we take our hands off of it.

When I called out to God, pleading with Him to make me securely attached to Him, He took me through a long process of discovering not only what was holding me back from enjoying this security but took me on a journey of discovering who He is. I have learned that God Himself is my complete safety, security, and home. I have learned that, come what may, nothing can snatch me out of His hands. I have cried for and over this deep inner healing. I have attended counseling sessions, prayer meetings, classes, and deliverance sessions. But the most important and deepest healing I have experienced in this area is in quiet moments alone with God in His presence as He has whispered to me, "You are mine. You will always be enough and you will always have enough, because you are mine."

One day in prayer, I heard in my spirit from God the words that I had been waiting to hear my entire life: "Your heart is fully secured to me." When I heard it, I ran to write it down. Could it be true? My heart? This heart? The one that had traveled the world and searched high and low for love and had always come up empty? The one that had tasted and tried all the world had to offer to attempt to gain emotional safety and had always come up dry? This heart, Lord?

The answer was subtle, and quiet, and still: "Yes." God had not only saved me physically, mentally, and spiritually, but He had answered the deepest cry of my heart by providing me the miracle of emotional security that I'd spent my lifetime searching for. And with that, I knew, and of course He knew, that I would never be the same.

9

Beauty For Ashes: God's Transforming Power

The Year of the Lord's Favor

The Spirit of the Sovereign Lord is on me,
because the Lord has anointed me
to proclaim good news to the poor.
He has sent me to bind up the brokenhearted,
to proclaim freedom for the captives
and release from darkness for the prisoners,
to proclaim the year of the Lord's favor
and the day of vengeance of our God,
to comfort all who mourn,
and provide for those who grieve in Zion—
to bestow on them a crown of beauty
instead of ashes,

> *the oil of joy*
> *instead of mourning,*
> *and a garment of praise*
> *instead of a spirit of despair.*
> *They will be called oaks of righteousness,*
> *a planting of the Lord*
> *for the display of his splendor.*

~ Isaiah 61:1-3

God's transformation of us is always an inside-out job. First we believe, and then He transforms, renews, and restores. We don't need to come to God neat and clean. We just need to come to Him. He will do the rest if we allow him. My mother told me long ago: "Melissa, as long as you walk with the Lord, I know you will always be okay." And my father told me: "This is the most important question to answer in life: 'Is my name written in The Lamb's Book of Life?'"

This has been the season in my life where God has restored me. He brought me peace, comfort, and safety where I had none. He took me from a place of complete brokenness, loss, and hopelessness, to a place of security, health, and abundant blessings.

Only God could have done this. Please know that while I submitted to Him, to His plan and path of deliverance and healing for me in every area of my life, I did so only as His Holy Spirit revealed it to me, one step at a time. Only God

Himself has brought this level of healing and restoration into my life.

God is best at taking nothing and making something brand-new and beautiful from it. "Forget the former things; do not dwell on the past. See, I am doing a new thing! Now it springs up; do you not perceive it? I am making a way in the wilderness and streams in the wasteland" (Isaiah 43:18-19). Look at all of creation around you. It all started with the Word. God spoke the world into being. "And God said, 'Let there be light,' and there was light" (Genesis 1:3).

We as people, who were created in God's image, can make many things happen in our own strength, but if we want the fullness of what God has planned for us to be manifested in our lives, we must be willing to submit to His will. God, in His grace and mercy, brought me to the end of myself. My stubbornness and pride have only served as a place of destruction in my life. But thank God that "The LORD is compassionate and gracious, slow to anger, and abounding in love" (Psalms 103:8).

In His great mercy, God allowed me to become desperate for Him through the realization that nothing I could do in my own strength was ever going to get me the kind of transformation I needed. Indeed, I have experienced and learned, "LORD, you establish peace for us; all that we have accomplished you have done for us" (Isaiah 26:12). God accomplished all through the death of His one and only Son, who was without sin and yet became sin and conquered sin and death when He rose from the grave. He took our place, so we don't have to pay the penalty for our transgressions. This is why Jesus is our very Prince of Peace.

In the midst of my deepest struggles and in the depths of my greatest suffering, I could have never known that this is how it would all work out. I only knew one thing: I had to hold onto Jesus. If only by the thread of His garment, if only touching the tip of His finger, if only stretching out as far as I had the strength—I never stopped reaching out for Him. Because not once has He ever stopped reaching out for me. The same goes for you. He's reaching out to you right now.

No matter where you are in this moment as you read this, no matter what your struggles, your fears, your battles, your sickness; I want you to know that Jesus has never, and will never, stop reaching out for you. He stands at the door and knocks. (Revelation 3:20). He's there now at the door of your very heart. If you would just open the door and let Him in, he will come in and sit down at your table. He will not rush away like so many others have, telling you that they have more important things to do.

No. He will linger with you. He will listen to you. He will talk with you. He will eat and drink with you. He will laugh with you. He will weep with you. And when you are all done, He will wipe away your tears and He will hold you close.

If you let Him, He will be the very best friend you've ever had. I know because He's been that for me. He's not only God. He's not only Lord. He's not only Savior. All power is given to my Best Friend.

Won't you consider this kind of friendship? I promise that you will not be disappointed. There are so many things I still don't fully understand about this friend of mine, but one thing He's never done is let me down. And I know He never will. He's reaching out to you now.

Romans 10:9 tells us: "That if you confess with your mouth the Lord Jesus and believe in your heart that God has raised Him from the dead, you will be saved." If you've never accepted Jesus into your heart, you can do so now by believing and praying this prayer out loud:

"Dear God, I want to be a part of your family. You said in Your Word that if I acknowledge that You raised Jesus from the dead and that I accept Him as my Lord and Savior, I would be saved. So God, I now say that I believe You raised Jesus from the dead and that He is alive and well. I accept Him now as my personal Lord and Savior. I accept my salvation from sin right now. I am now saved. Jesus is my Lord. Jesus is my Savior. Thank you, Father God, for forgiving me, saving me, and giving me eternal life with You. Amen!"

10

Unending Blessings And Many Rooms: Learning To Abide And Trust

In my Father's house are many mansions:
if it were not so, I would have told you.
I go to prepare a place for you.

~ John 14:2

So much of my journey has really been about learning to trust God. Learning to trust Him in the mountaintop experiences and in the valleys. Learning to trust Him along every step of the journey of life that He has given me. My father once told me that God asks us the same question every day: "Will you trust me?"

Almost exactly one year ago, in May 2019, about one week before I cried out to God for further healing and He answered me by saying: "You are going to write your way through this," I was taking a walk with my dog, Sherman, in Portland Maine. It was a drizzly, raw, and cold morning, which is not uncommon for Maine, but nonetheless a bit depressing in mid-May. I was feeling a bit tired and lacking hope and motivation. I started to feel that all-too-familiar empty feeling deep in my chest and my stomach. I started praying and asking Jesus to come in and fill all the empty places inside of me with Himself. And then He began to speak.

This is what Holy Spirit revealed to me: "You must remember that you are currently living in two realities: This physical reality on earth and the spiritual reality in Heaven. Both are just as real for you right now, but what you see here on earth is overcome by me. 'Take heart for I have overcome the world.' What you need to remember is that it was for 'the joy set before ME, that I endured the cross.' This joy was you. To know that I would be with you forever in eternity and there would be no separation between YOU and ME. This is the same joy set before you, that you must cling to now, in this physical realm. I stepped out of eternity and became flesh, and confined myself to physical space and time, so you would have my mind—THE MIND of CHRIST—NOW. Even now in this physical realm, I died so you could live in the physical, while being conscious of this spiritual reality. Although your body is currently confined to physical space and time, you can operate in the spiritual, heavenly realms and reality, because you have MY MIND. In ME, all was created and has its being, and all holds together in ME. Nothing was created or has its being apart from, or is held together apart from me. All the creation groans to be reconciled to ME. Like a bud that does not flower overnight, but takes time in this physical reality to go through it's a process of unfolding and blossoming, so do you take time in your process of becoming who I have created you to be. You see this occurring over time and become impatient because you are living in the reality of physical time, but in the reality of eternity with ME, it has all already occurred. Hold on to these truths, and seek ME. Seek Rest, Peace, Joy, and Love in and through me, as you wait to see revealed what I have already done in the spiritual realm."

I have now seen performed and manifested through the writing of this book in the physical what the Spirit of God prophesized to my spirit one year ago. It is now May 2020, and we are in the midst of a global pandemic, but God's word for me for 2020, "Release," is being manifested in my life even now. I am currently making plans to step out in faith and follow God to a job that He has called me to teach in South Carolina. God is sovereign and nothing that is occurring in this physical world can stop His plans and purpose that He has for your life if you but follow Him in trust, faith, and obedience.

God shared with me in early January of 2020: With every promotion and acceleration, the enemy's tactic will be to try to cause you to feel anxious and overwhelmed. He wants to take God's breakthroughs and blessings in your life and distort them into burdens. The Lord told me how to avoid this: With each breakthrough, blessing, and acceleration, immediately lay it back down at the foot of the cross and give it back to God. Surrender each one back to Him, and the enemy can't get hold of it, or your mind!

This season is about God wanting to take your focus off of the past and put your focus on the future that He has planned for you. This season is about God breaking the yolk from the past and your history of living your life under threat, guilt, and shame, and instead creating a brand-new mind and heart that's full of expectancy and joy for the future! God wants you to take your focus off the past and everything that you think you've lost and put it on the future and everything that He's about to do.

Very recently, while I was walking in the woods and gazing around at the flowers and plants coming to life in springtime, God's Spirit spoke to me: "There is so much beauty to be had, seen, and experienced in this time of transition. Submit all of the details of this transition to Me. Do not rush toward the outcome, but rather enjoy the unfolding. Be still and peaceful during this time of transition. Look around you at how nature transitions from one state to another. Look how I created it to be so. So it is with you. I am in control of every detail. Submit and commit all details of this transition to me. If I have met your needs in the depths of winter, how much more can you be sure that I will meet your needs in the transition between winter and spring, and in between spring and summer, and in between summer and fall?"

What God has for you is *for you*. There was purpose in everything you have walked through to arrive at this moment. Everything served its purpose. Everything. Be gracious. God has used all for your good. Even the betrayals, the bitter defeats, the disappointments, the losses, each one of these served a purpose to mold you into the person whom God has called you to become. Where is the fault of grievances to forgive then, when looking through God's eyes of Love, when understanding things from God's perspective? It was good for you to be afflicted. All of it brought you to this moment. The only appropriate response, then, is gratitude.

It is important to recognize that, in order to abide in God and trust in Him, we have to break off past resentments and sources of bitterness and rejections. They might be professional or personal but, if we don't break them off, we are going to put this brokenness from our pasts onto the new things that God wants to do in our lives. We have to recognize that what the enemy meant for harm, the Lord meant for good. What you saw as rejection was actually God's protection.

So take the time right now to command and cast out the spirit of rejection, the spirit of bitterness, the spirit of resentment, the spirit of false responsibility, the spirit of guilt, the spirit of distrust, the spirit of fear of punishment, the spirit of fear, the spirit of anxiety, and the spirit of depression, the spirit of striving, the spirit of performance, the spirit of judgment, and the spirit of criticism. These spirits are evil and will work toward your demise.

We must fight the plague of fear that is attempting to infect and overwhelm our lives. We must command and cast out all thoughts of doubt, trouble, anxiety, and worry at the very first sign of them in our minds because these thoughts are thieves that attempt to steal the treasures within you that God has deposited in your spirit. We must command and cast out the spirit of rehearsal that would tempt us to go over past wrongdoings and mistakes again and again, along with the spirit of magnification, that would tempt us to have our minds distort life issues into catastrophic events.

This aspect of our healing journey might hurt emotionally, psychologically, spiritually, and even physically, as God teaches us to lay everything down at the foot of the cross, but we cannot expect to walk into what God has for us next in the physical without going through the inner spiritual growth pains.

Therefore, we replace these spirits with the Mind of Christ, the Peace of Christ, the Comfort of Christ, the Perfect Supply of Christ, the Validation of Christ, and the Ultimate

Security of Christ. Fear has no place. The perfect love of God casts out all fear!

In this next season, you are not going to be able to hide anymore. God is going to bring you fully into His body and fully into the intimacy as the Body of Christ with other believers. In order for God to do this, you must allow Him to break off the spirits of rejection, past resentments, and bitterness, in order to step fully into the newness of relationship and community that God has for you in this next season both professionally and personally.

You don't have to protect yourself anymore, beloved. You don't have to try to keep yourself safe. Jesus is here. He's going to keep you safe. You can trust again. You can trust Him and you can trust others. It's okay. Your heart is safe now. You can let go. The more of ourselves we surrender to God, the more He can use us.

Claim things with Divine Audacity now! Anything and everything is yours in Christ! He's going to put a new song in your mouth! He's going to take the broken things and make them beautiful! He's going to restore all you lost! He's going to rewrite your story! Just be still and know that He is God. Entrust your heart and life fully into His care. Trust in God leads to calm, which leads to peace, which leads to joy.

Not only does God save us, He secures us and directs us, but as we abide in Him and trust in Him, He promises also to keep our very way secure that He has directed us in. Psalms

18:32: "It is God Who arms me with strength, and makes my way secure." I have seen the promise of Psalms 18:19 in my own life: "He brought me out into a spacious place; He rescued me because he delighted in me."

I want to encourage you, dear reader, that there is so much beauty waiting for you in your life to come. I can testify to the power of our God to take ashes and create beauty. Please humble yourself before God, because he *will* lift you up. "Blessed is the one who perseveres under trial because, having stood the test, that person will receive the crown of life that the Lord has promised to those who love him" (James 1:12).

The best is yet to come for you in the Lord: "Arise, shine, for your light has come, and the glory of the LORD rises upon you" (Isaiah 60:1).

THE VINE AND THE BRANCHES

"I am the true vine, and my Father is the gardener. [2] He cuts off every branch in me that bears no fruit, while every branch that does bear fruit he prunes so that it will be even more fruitful. [3] You are already clean because of the word I have spoken to you. [4] Remain in me, as I also remain in you. No branch can bear fruit by itself; it must remain in the vine. Neither can you bear fruit unless you remain in me.

[5] "I am the vine; you are the branches. If you remain in me and I in you, you will bear much fruit; apart from me you can do nothing. [6] If you do not remain in me, you are like a branch that is thrown away and withers; such branches are picked up, thrown into the fire and burned. [7] If you remain in me and my words remain in you, ask whatever you wish, and it will be done for you. [8] This is to my Father's glory, that you bear much fruit, showing yourselves to be my disciples.

[9] "As the Father has loved me, so have I loved you. Now remain in my love. [10] If you keep my commands, you will remain in my love, just as I have kept my Father's commands and remain in his love. [11] I have told you this so that my joy may be in you and that your joy may be complete. [12] My command is this: Love each other as I have loved you. [13] Greater love has no one than this: to lay down one's life for one's friends. [14] You are my friends if you do what I command. [15] I no longer call you servants, because a servant does not know his master's business. Instead, I have called you friends, for everything that I learned from my Father I have made known to you. [16] You did not choose me, but I chose you and appointed you so that you might go and bear fruit—fruit that will last— and so that whatever you ask in my name the Father will give you. [17] This is my command: Love each other. (John 15:1-17).

Let's remain in our Best Friend's Love. Let's let Him Love us into Loving ourselves. Let's Love each other as He has Loved us—with a heart fully secured in Christ.

REFERENCES

Ben-Shahar, T. (2007). *Happier: Learn the Secrets to Daily Joy and Lasting Fulfillment.* McGraw-   Hill.

Cloud, H. & Townsend, J. (1992). *Boundaries: When to Say Yes, How to Say No, To Take Control*

of Your Life. Zondervan.

L'Engle, M. (2001). *Walking on Water: Reflections on Faith and Art.* Waterbrook Press.

Smith, H. W. (1956). *The God of All Comfort.* Moody Publishers.

Walsh, S. (2011) *The Shelter of God's Promises.* Thomas Nelson.